WHAT W

I Married ~~a man with Triplets...~~

To
Marcie
Thank you
for reading - Hope
you enjoy! Lynette Moore

WHAT WAS I THINKING?

I Married a Man with Triplets!!!

Lynette Moore

What Was I Thinking?

I Married a Man with Triplets!!!

Printed in the U.S.A.

Book design by Brian Moreland

ISBN: 978-0-578-33451-6

Author's Note: While this is a memoir based on a period of my life, some people's names have been changed to fictional names.

To Jim, a wonderful husband
and father of seven beautiful boys.

One

Have any of you ever tried internet dating? Well, I have! For a single woman, online dating is the easiest way to meet prospective husbands if you live in a small town and you are the *only* single woman in the community (well, not exactly, but often times it seemed that way).

Back in 1998, I lived in Colorado City, also known as "The Heart of West Texas." It was a nice small town and somewhere you would enjoy living and raising your children, if you were married and had a family. It was also a good place to live if you were single and wanted to spend the rest of your life by yourself. Does that sound great? Well, not to me!

At the time, I was a single mom, worked as a school teacher, taught piano lessons, and served as music director at the First United Methodist Church. On top of all that, I was miserably lonely. I had not had much luck in the area of marriage.

I married my first husband, Jerry, when I was young. We had one son, Derek, together, but Jerry and I ended up getting divorced. I was a single mom for about twelve years and was ready for my relationship drought to end. I married my second husband, George, in 1992 and we had a son together, Sam. One day, after working overseas as a drilling supervisor, George arrived back in the States and stopped to see his family and friends in his hometown before traveling home to Colorado

City. George suddenly died of a massive heart attack. He was only 41!

I was devastated. I could only try to explain to my youngest son, Sam, who was only three, that his father had gone to Heaven. We were already struggling financially, so I immediately started a house cleaning business on the side. I still taught piano lessons, acted as music director at my church, and did my best to keep my head above water, both financially and emotionally.

Even though I had remained good friends with my first husband, Jerry, he passed away, too, in 1998. Our son, Derek, was just about to graduate high school and planned to attend Texas Tech in Lubbock. Having lost both fathers to my sons and been left a widow by George, I felt like maybe I was cursed.

After enduring another five years of being a single parent in a small town, I decided to venture into the internet dating scene. I could write another book just on *that* adventure! I created my profile, uploaded photos, and got ready for Mr. Right to email me. My friends and family were encouraging, telling me, "Maybe the third time's the charm." I sure hoped so.

I met some very nice men, fell in love a few times, and actually had some great experiences. However, my heart could only be broken so many times, and after five years of dating, something had to give. I felt frustrated and neglected. I decided to take a break from any contacts or communication. I needed a reprieve to regain my willingness to continue the search. I had to get some clarity on what traits I really wanted in a spouse. Believe me, the online dating scene can certainly curb your values…sometimes to a fault.

During that recess from the internet, I asked the only other single person in town to go out on a dinner date. He was a member of the choir at church, and I thought we might have a chance for a little romance. We were leaving from rehearsal at the same time one evening and met in the parking lot. I asked him to come to my house for dinner, and then he spent 30 minutes lecturing me about why dating me wasn't a good idea. Okay, scratch off the last single man in my zip code.

By 2001, I was worried I might never find Mr. Right, but I was willing to give internet matchmaking another shot. So I resumed my online search. I needed the extra ego boost I acquired when I turned on the computer first thing in the morning (or the middle of the night) and saw that some poor soul out there in cyberspace had shown an interest in my measly attempt to post a profile. Soon, men emailed me and I was off and running again, bracing my heart for more disappointments and heartaches.

This time, I took a different approach. Right up front on my profile I boldly explained that my former husband had passed and I was a widow raising an eight-year-old son. I also mentioned that I had another son with my first husband (who was also dead), and that my oldest son was attending Texas Tech. My profile stated that I did not smoke or drink, and that church was very important to me. I was looking for a Christian husband who enjoyed going to church and doing volunteer work and had strong family values. I quickly discovered that too much criteria lessened the chance of a perfect match, but it also weeded out many of the men who were not prime prospects. I was tired of messing around, wasting time, and chasing impossible dreams. I wanted a man close to my age, and who did not mind the fact that I had a child.

That type of man was hard to find! If they were middle-aged, then their children were almost grown and they were not willing to take on raising another young child. If they were much older, then they were "okay" with children because they considered them the same as grandchildren.

Still, there was a problem. After a few months of dating,

the men realized that this child was not going home to his parents like other grandchildren. Sam was already home, and that piece of information did not settle well with the older generation. At this stage of the game, the chances of finding Mr. Right were about as good as winning the lottery. I had pretty much lost hope, but still enjoyed the thought of *just maybe…* And remember, of all that, I was downright lonely.

Just a few days after I posted my very last profile qualifying myself as "truly a rare breed," I received an email from a man in Lubbock:

Hi Lynette,

You do indeed appear to be a rare breed!

I am 54, an attorney at Texas Tech as well as a Magistrate. I have custody (currently shared custody) of my three six-year-old boys. I know, I know…what was I thinking?? Actually, they are the joy of my life. Parenthood is so much more fun this time around.

I am also active in my church. I was co-chair of the last stewardship campaign and I am currently co-chairman of a capital campaign that is going on. I like to keep fit. I play basketball 3 times a week at the rec center on campus. The other days I do cardio or light weights. I am 5'11", 180 pounds. I don't have a profile posted on this service. I can send a photo if anything here sparks an interest. I just don't know how to attach a photo in this first message box. If you would like to talk, email me at my hotmail address and I will then send the photo.

Jim

Three red flags flew up!

Triplets? That was it. He was history. No more communication. This one was dead in the water, no question about it.

"Pretend he never wrote," I told myself. "Wipe him off the list and move on to the next."

Why couldn't I have listened to what I was saying? Why did I write him back?

What was I thinking?

I was thinking, *This man is a Christian, an attorney, and I just love smart men!*

I'll be honest, as a struggling single mother, I wanted someone financially stable, a good father figure for Sam, and chemistry was a must. Here he was, on my screen, providing just enough tantalizing information to tempt me. I *had* to find out more, but oh, my...

Triplets!!!

Obviously, he had subscribed to the dating service, but opted not to post a profile. Another red flag immediately flew up. I thought he might still be married. I did not like someone knowing more about me than I knew about him; but this was a challenge and I loved challenges. I could not resist. After all, he was an attorney!

I wrote back. I was a little intimidated, because he had all the information he needed to know at that particular point from my profile. It was time for me to ask the questions. So I asked for information that I figured he was obviously not willing to give. He not only willingly replied, he explained why his profile was not posted, and he supplied me with all the information I needed to stay interested.

Jim had been divorced for three years. He grew up in O'Donnell, Texas, a small town near Lubbock, and acquired his law degree from Texas Tech. He had practiced for many years but had given that up when the triplets were born to keep from traveling. He was now the Director of the Student Mediation Center at Texas Tech University in Lubbock, and was enjoying a more simple life rather than the fast-paced life of a civil defense lawyer.

Over the next few days, Jim proved too good to be true. He sent a picture of him and the triplets that the church newspaper had used for a story on Father's Day. He was gorgeous, charming, and intelligent. He was very interesting and seemed perfect except for those three red flags plus an ex-wife living in the same town. I knew I was asking for trouble, and all along, I kept telling myself, "I am *not* going to fall in love with this man."

My mother had always said, "Don't ever date a man you would not consider marrying." Did I ever listen? I kept thinking, *What's the harm?* We were just emailing and the communication seemed harmless enough. After all, I was never going meet this man or fall in love with him. He had triplets. I was still thinking, right?

Against my better judgment, we kept communicating. Jim seemed so different from all the rest of the men I had met on the internet. He was so gentle and kind. He was charming and did not have a touch of arrogance in his bones. We all know lawyers are known to have overblown egos, but not this one. His father worked as a tenant farmer until Jim was twelve. Later, his father bought a country grocery store in Draw, Texas and the family lived in a small house behind the store. Jim grew up as a small-town boy with small-town values. I thought I wanted to be taken away from all that and find a rich man in a big city. No wonder I had it set in my mind that I was *never* going to meet this man, much less fall in love with him.

He soon started sending me love poems. How could I turn away from this amazing man? I had not even met him. Not only did he have triplets, I soon learned that he had two older sons from a previous marriage. Five sons!

At this point, I was pretty sure I wasn't thinking clearly. This is when I decided I needed extra help and guidance. Do you have a precious aunt? Well, I do, and her name is Aunt Mollie. Aunt Mollie Pearl to be exact. And, she is a work of art. She is my mentor, confidant, and best friend. She knows all and speaks all; advises me on everything. She has been my cheerleader in the internet search and has readily shared opinions on things (and prospective husbands), even if I didn't want to hear them. Aunt Mollie loves me and has always wanted the best for me. I love her very much, too, and have always listened to everything she said.

When I told her about Jim and the triplets, she became very vivid. She pointed out what his house must look like… how there would be no walking space because of all the toys… how the two-car garage would not possibly have room for two cars, and how the laundry room would be full of dirty clothes. She explained everyday life with triplets, including details like swiping and sharing germs on toothpaste tubes and creating multiple science fair projects for school. Lord knows how she knew; she has never even had one child. However, she spoke, so I listened and began to form a very colorful picture of what life would be like with this man, which was okay because I was never going to meet him anyway.

At this point, Jim and I were still emailing through the dating service. He had given me his hotmail address but there was a glitch and he did not receive one of my responses. He did not answer back and I thought for some reason he had lost interest. From online-dating experience, I figured he was getting back with the mother of his children or he had found someone else. That was fine because I still had some old and new contacts, and I was still seeing a rich man in a big city. Unfortunately, he had custody of two teenage sons and chose to only see me when the boys were gone. That was not enough for me. Also, it was a three-hour drive to the city, and long-distance dating is for the birds.

By now, I realized I was captivated by Jim's interest in me and not just his boys. I was very intrigued, but I knew ending the relationship before it really started was for the best. Thank God I was still thinking.

But was I? Days passed and I could not help myself. What was wrong with me? In his last email, he said he was getting excited. I found myself writing him again at the old address. Here is what I wrote:

Hi Jim,

I don't want to seem pretentious, but I sent this to your Hotmail address and was not sure you received it. I would like to think, after your last statement, that you are interested enough to write back. I was wondering why you had not responded.

Lynette

His response was almost immediate. As I read what he wrote, my thinking began to get a little cloudy.

Hello Lynette,

What a pleasant surprise to find your note!! I was afraid that I had scared you. I did not get your message to Hotmail. I tried to send you a message from that address but it was undeliverable because that address is not registered with the dating service. Way too complicated for me!

I want this fledgling relationship to progress at the pace you want. There is no hurry, just a sense of excitement. That is okay, it is what makes new experiences fun!! There are sites in Colorado City to see... you are there!

Thinking of you.
Jim

Oh, no! In one of our previous emails, he had hinted about coming to Colorado City to see the sights, and I quickly told him there were no sights to see. There was no reason at all for him to come to Colorado City. I did not intend to ever meet Jim, and I was not going to fall in love with him.

PART ONE

Dating Mr. Right

Two

It was not long before he planned a weekend to come to Colorado City while the triplets were with their mother. I tried desperately to discourage him. I told him that weekend I had already planned a surprise birthday party for an elderly couple that I house-cleaned for. The man lived at home, but his wife was in a wheelchair in the local nursing home. The element of surprise was going to take some manipulation and I did not know if I could handle that *and* entertaining a strange man at the same time. We were also having vacation Bible school at church, and Friday was the final night. I was the music director and directed the children's choir, so naturally I played a large part in the production. On top of everything else, Sam had another birthday party he was invited to, and somehow I had to manage transportation for him to and from the party and then to VBS at church. I was also in the process of painting my kitchen…by myself.

Jim and I had decided it would need to be an overnight trip. Friday was not good for me. Saturday was not good for Jim because he always picked up the triplets from their mother's to take them to church on Sunday morning. Reluctantly, I told him if he wanted to go ahead and come, he could follow me around and see what my life was all about. I also told him if he would wait for another weekend (or maybe for the rest of my life), he would have my full attention. Of course, it was his choice. I figured he would choose the latter, but he decided he was coming Friday! I said okay. I need to mention here that I am always a sucker, a pushover, a patsy.

Jim called and said he would like to get here around 10:00 a.m. on Friday and I almost choked on clean air. No way! So, he was taking off work? Never in my life have I ever taken off work on a Friday just because I wanted to meet a potential future spouse.

What is he thinking?

I was trying to paint kitchen cabinets, make final preparations for the vacation Bible school finale, organize a surprise birthday party for my client, and I still needed to pick up a present for Sam's friend's birthday party and get it wrapped. If Jim came Friday morning, then I would have to prepare lunch too? I don't think so… Thank goodness, dinner was covered. I was ordering pizza to be delivered at the elderly couple's house.

I got an email from Jim early Friday morning. At 6:15 a.m., he wrote that he had been dressed, packed, and ready to leave for an hour. It was at least a two-hour drive from his house to mine, so I wrote back, "Wait!"

At 9:00 a.m., he emailed back that he was leaving: he could not wait any longer, but would wait to call until about noon. Thank God for that.

Something was working to my benefit because he did not call until almost 1:00 that afternoon. He had missed the exit to Colorado City and ended up in Sweetwater. That little mistake cost him almost two hours, and needless to say, I was not impressed. Was this man really as intelligent as I'd first thought? Hmmm… I started wondering.

Lunch had been ready for almost an hour when Jim finally called from the local motel. At passing intervals, I thought I had been stood up, which would not have been the first time. Dating comes with lots of experiences, including being stood up, but this was the first time someone had gotten lost. I was nervous.

At 1:15, the doorbell rang and my heart jumped up in my throat. What was wrong with me? I was not going to fall in love with this guy. But then again, I was never going to meet him either, right?

Well, here I go…

I opened the door and there he was, perfectly dressed in pressed navy slacks and collared shirt. And very handsome. His brown eyes twinkled. He carried a single red rose in his right hand for me and a book in his left hand for Sam. Jim was not exactly what I expected.

Those of you who have dated online have witnessed men who claimed to be six-foot tall and 180 pounds. Face to face, they turn out to be five-eight and weigh 200 plus. Jim was real. He had claimed to be five-ten and 180 pounds. He was all that. Did I mention he was gorgeous? I was swooning.

I accepted the rose he offered and headed to the kitchen to find a vase. He followed. I teased Jim about missing the exit, and his response looking at me with those twinkling eyes: "It just gave me more time to think about finally meeting you."

I melted.

Ever since Sam was about six years old, I had shared most of the online connections I had made with him. Sam was my best friend, and he was always ready to put in his two cents.

"Mom, he looks so old!"

"He's almost bald!"

"Does he have any kids my age?"

Sam and I both wanted a father who wouldn't die on us. I wanted a husband, and acquiring three brothers were more than what Sam could hope for. Here Jim was, checking off all of the traits above and standing in my kitchen.

I tried to stay calm, but my heart was pounding. I remember standing at the sink in front of the window, filling tea glasses, and almost in a breathtaking sigh he said, "You are beautiful."

My knees became weak and I began to tremble. My face was hot. Like a schoolgirl, I was blushing. This near-perfect man had come straight from my dreams, but the triplets were still very real.

I placed our sandwiches on plates, and we sat at the table. He looked at me and offered his hand. I put mine in his, and together we bent our heads as he started praying. I was astonished. Never had I witnessed this kind of spirituality since I was a girl at home with my family. My Father always prayed before meals. It was so comforting to know that Jim had this same Christian value.

About halfway through lunch, we started talking about the complicated plans for the afternoon and evening. I had been cleaning Marge and Lucky's house for about a year, and they had adopted me as one of their own. Marge had been moved to a nursing home about three months earlier, but had wanted to surprise Lucky with a birthday party at their house. She had asked me to help organize it. The only way it would work would be for Jim to pick up Marge and her wheelchair from the nursing home and take her to their house, while I took Lucky and Sam out for a diversion. Of course, this seemed outrageous since Jim had never met these two people or the guests that were coming to the party. Jim was not deterred. I would take Sam on to his birthday party, and then when Lucky and I returned to their house, we would all shout "Happy Birthday" and eat pizza. As I was explaining the situation, Jim was all ears and eager to help. That's the first time I really saw deeply into his twinkling eyes, and the twinkle was for me!

Timing was critical. Soon after pizza and presents, I would need to leave to get ready for the vacation Bible study finale. There was a small window of opportunity to pick up Sam and get him to the production. We left Marge at the house and told her we would return later to take her back to the nursing home.

At vacation Bible school, I was also involved in the crafts section, since I also managed the Kids Club (an afterschool program for working parents). We had forty kids to supervise painting tee-shirts, and Jim was amazing. As if knowing what to do, he jumped right in and had those kids designing and creating. I guess there are some advantages of having experience with kids; I just had not considered getting hooked up with a father of five sons. This was mind-boggling.

I must say, Jim was a real trooper. I put him to the test that day. I had him picking up old women from nursing homes, carting kids to and from birthday parties, dealing with children armed with paintbrushes and sponges, and meeting the whole congregation of the First United Methodist Church (my family), all in one evening. When we finally arrived at my house later that night, I was exhausted. I got Sam to bed and joined Jim on the couch in the living room. We talked about the day. He laughed at himself missing the exit and ending up in Sweetwater. We both felt very happy about the success of the birthday party, and how the vacation Bible study program had been a hit.

Feeling sleepy, I yawned.

Jim rose from the couch. "I'd better go."

I walked him to the door and he turned and took me into his arms. I melted. I looked into his eyes and said, "Thank you so much for all your help. You are amazing."

At that point he took both sides of my face in his hands and gave me the most wonderful, tender, energized kiss I had ever felt.

He said, "I'll see you in the morning," and then he left to stay the night at a hotel.

I stood at the entrance, stunned and happy.

* * *

As a runner, I had developed the habit of getting up early. I often ran before daylight while Sam slept. Since Jim played basketball three times a week, he thought he might like to take up running too, something we could enjoy together. I was leery when Jim said he would join me Saturday morning. Remember, this is our first weekend together. I had told him I would call when I was almost ready to run. As his phone was ringing, I saw lights in my driveway. He was there, ready and willing, tennis shoes and all. I usually jogged four or five miles, but I decided to go easy on him that morning. We ran two miles, and I was totally impressed. He did not pass out or throw up. He passed the test.

After we cooled down a bit in my kitchen, he left to go back to his hotel room, get dressed, and pack up to leave. When he got back to my house, we had a nice leisurely breakfast and began planning our next rendezvous. It was going to be a while before we could see each other again, because I was leaving the next day to go visit my wise Aunt Mollie for a week. Jim and I agreed to keep in touch while I was in Austin.

I would say our first meeting was quite a success. Unlike some of the other internet prospects, I actually enjoyed Jim being around. However, he had come alone this time. Who knows what would have happened had he been waving three red flags when he and his triplets piled out of his more than conventional mini-van. At that point, I would have locked the doors and closed the blinds. I should have anyway. What was I thinking?

* * *

That very afternoon I received an email from Jim:

Subject: What a Great Visit

Lynette, I can't tell you how nice these past 1-½ days have been. It felt like home. I know you still have the boys to meet and they may seem like quite a challenge. Lynette, I like you. You inspire me to do better than I am. Running.... me??

On the way home, I listened to a song by Alan Jackson, "When Love Comes Around." It said just what I was feeling. Neither of us knows what the future may bring, but that song spoke to me. Listen to it sometime.

Back to real,
Jim

I drove as fast as I could to Austin. I was anxious to tell Aunt Mollie and Uncle Dee all about this new, interesting man that I was not going to fall in love with. I knew they could offer a clear perspective and ease my mind. Aunt Mollie would remind me of what his house probably looked like, and how difficult it would be to live in the same town with the triplets' mother. Uncle Dee could throw a light on the practical subjects of teenagers, cars, grocery bills, and college. Aunt Mollie can be handy in times of need…and I desperately needed a confidant to keep me thinking straight. My aunt and uncle were the ticket.

While I was in Austin, Jim and I kept corresponding. He called a few times. He knew my son, Derek, was a student at

Texas Tech University, so Jim graciously gifted him an airline ticket to join us for a visit in Austin. My oldest sister, Carole, and my mom, Dorothy, also joined us for a small family reunion. I had all the support necessary to convince me I did not need to be a stepmom to triplets, much less five boys! We all gathered in Aunt Mollie and Uncle Dee's study. Carole began to talk about all the advantages of having a large family.

There are four children in my family and we are all very close, even though there is an age span of sixteen years. Carole is the oldest, then Caye is five years younger. I follow two and a half years later, and then our younger brother, Scott, is eight years younger than me. We have all made an effort to stay close and connected through thick and thin.

As we were congregated in the study, Carole said, "Think about it…" She went on to tell me our new family would always have our own baseball team at picnics. We could get massive family discounts at amusement parks and have our own pew at church. There would always be enough people to play board games, even if someone did not want to play. And I could buy bulk quantities of food and know it would not go to waste. I would have my own yard crew and live-in car wash. Carole actually thought it would be fun having so many kids around the same age. I had also thought about Sam and how he would never be bored or lonely again with three younger brothers.

Carole said, "You can do it!"

I responded, "Why would I want to?"

She grinned. "To get the man."

My oldest son, Derek, listened to all the pros and cons, I could see thoughts forming in his mind. Later, as I took him to the airport to fly back to Lubbock, I asked him to give me his thoughts.

He gently said, "Mom, I just want you to be happy."

His father had died when Derek was a senior in high

school, and we had both felt the pain and the overwhelming loss. *Just be happy.* His advice still lives in my heart today.

*   *   *

Sam and I left Austin on Saturday so I could be back on Sunday to fulfill my duties as choir director. I was very confused. I was sad to leave the comfort I get from being at Aunt Mollie and Uncle Dee's, but I was anxious to see what the next chapter in my life had in store for me. Uncle Dee knew. After I left, he told Aunt Mollie I was going to marry that man. She asked how he knew, and he told her because Jim was the main subject and everything was positive. He also knew I could handle triplets if I had the desire. I felt certain I did not have the desire, nor did have the courage! But then again, I wanted to be happy.

Three

As I settled into being back in Colorado City again, I began resuming my internet search for amazing matches. I no longer felt the excitement of getting a new match. I lacked the motivation to start a conversation with a potential prospect. Jim and I had begun corresponding regularly, and I suddenly quit getting up in the middle of the night just to see if some poor soul had shown interest in my profile. A few online suitors trickled in, but Jim continued to mesmerize me, and I wanted to know more about him. My replies to eligible prospects began to be few and far between.

Jim called occasionally, but most of our correspondence was online. We emailed regularly and discovered Instant Messaging. This type of communication was very accommodating, because it allowed time for me to think before responding. He had also been sending me handwritten poems…love poems, about me.

As the weekend approached, Jim invited me to come and meet the triplets.

What? Already? It seemed too soon.

I had dated some men with children, but I was never allowed to meet them. I thought, *This is a brave man. Surely, he would want me to get to know him a little better before he splattered me with reality.*

Jim invited Sam and me to come on Saturday morning and spend the day. He wanted to get to know Sam better, and for me to meet the triplets. Was Jim nuts? I could not believe he was comfortable with the situation. It seemed so unreal. What was he thinking? I needed time to think about this. I needed to consult Aunt Mollie, Carole, and Derek again. What if I went to Jim's and the day turned out perfect? What if he was a gracious host and the triplets were adorable? Then, I would take a step back, and the dark side of Jim's family would creep in. I could picture their house—the mess. I imagined this man trying to cook dinner for us with all these kids creating pure bedlam. You see, I was still thinking.

On Friday morning, I called Derek to get his input. He is the sweetest, kindest, human being on earth. He told me, "Do what makes you happy, Mom. If you don't go and see, you will never know." Such wise words from a young soul.

After much thought and consideration, that same morning, I called Jim and told him we would come. We talked about the visit and decided what to do while we were there. We both agreed it would be easier to stay at his home instead of trying to go out for lunch or dinner. So you understand? He was planning to cook dinner. This, I just had to see!

Sam was excited. He could not wait to meet the boys. Right away, he started planning what all he could take and how he could entertain three six-year-olds all day. He loved the idea of having a captive audience. He would never admit it, but I knew he could hardly wait to be the center of attention. And if he played his cards right, they would do exactly what he told them all day long.

Sam and I had been involved in Boy Scouts, and he had recently experienced the feeling of leadership. He was in Heaven. He would soon be able to try out his leadership skills on three unsuspecting little boys.

* * *

Even though Sam was ready to leave at 8:00 a.m., I procrastinated, so we arrived at Jim's house at about noon. It was a ranch style house, well kept, and probably built in the '70s. The yard was manicured, and there were no real signs of anything out of the ordinary. I pulled up in the driveway and, within seconds, the front door opened. Out flew the male population of the Albright household! One, two, three, four… yes, they were all there. Everyone was smiling, happy, warm, clean, and apparently ready for company. We stood outside on the driveway for a few minutes while I tried to let everything soak in. The children were almost overwhelming. The triplets were so enamored with Sam, and he was so excited to show them what all he had brought for their entertainment.

Jim gave me a casual hug and his eyes sparkled…again.

Everyone felt very comfortable with the situation except for me, because I was wondering how I allowed myself to get into this situation. It was still just a day visit. Nothing wrong with that.

Everyone grabbed something from the car and we migrated into the house. I could only imagine why the garage doors were closed, so we entered through the front door. Very nice! The main living area was very neat, clean, and tidy. No toys on the floor to have to step over. No distinct smell of abundant testosterone. I was amazed.

Jim had lunch ready with great preparations for sandwiches—whole wheat bread, deli lunchmeats, carrot sticks, and chips. Milk for the boys and diet cokes for us. I still felt uncomfortable and nervous, but Jim was holding up splendidly. He expertly fixed sandwiches for himself and his three boys, and I fixed one for Sam and me. It was pretty chaotic, but manageable. We let the boys eat outside, which would give us a chance to eat in peace at the kitchen table.

Well, that was a good idea, but not very realistic. We were dealing with three six-year-olds, an eight-year-old, and all boys. Did we really think they would all sit outside, quietly eat and give us some peace? We were dreaming.

The boys were excited and full of energy, and eating was the last thing on their minds. We tried to ignore them, but the back door probably opened sixteen times within ten minutes, making it difficult for Jim and I to carry on a conversation. We gave up, hurriedly finished our sandwiches, and headed outside. We figured if we were outside, too, the need to come in and out of the house would cease.

What a mess! There was food everywhere. On the table, on the chairs, spilled milk…everywhere there was evidence of a picnic gone awry. I helped Jim clean up and noticed his eyes still sparkled, in spite of the chaos. If this date were at my house, I would have been embarrassed, but he was handling the mess graciously. He smiled through it and never apologized for the boys' behavior. At this time, I was in complete denial that Sam could have done anything to add to the behavior. Not my child…this was obviously all the triplets' doings.

Once the newness wore off that day, everyone settled down a bit. Sam had brought some golf clubs with harmless plastic golf balls, and they stayed busy seeing who could knock them over the fence. No telling how many balls we lost that day. I don't think the triplets had ever laid eyes on golf clubs or balls. The game entertained the boys for a while, but after they grew weary of golf, they played on the swing set, ran dump trucks into each other, and got along splendidly. Sam was learning how to play them, and so far, the triplets all seemed to enjoy letting him be the boss. Meanwhile, Jim and I tried to get to know each other better.

For dinner, Jim took charge of cooking on outside on the grill: hamburgers for us and hot dogs for the kids. My job was easy because I was only in charge of the bread and condiments. Jim looked like a pro standing in front of the grill. Since we had learned our lesson over the lunch ordeal, we decided to all sit together at his kitchen table, which comfortably seated six. It was a good thing that Jim and I had been able to visit some that afternoon, because there was no way to get a word in edgewise at dinnertime. All the boys talked at once, striving to be heard…except for Cody. He was quiet, barely eating, and hardly looked up. I was intrigued by the dark-headed, brown-eyed young boy. Cooper and Caleb behaved differently, both fully involved in the conversation. I quickly figured out what role each triplet took. Cooper was the leader of the pack, and a little bossy. Caleb was the people pleaser, and Cody just went with the flow.

As dinner proceeded, I noticed that no one had set the table with silverware. Since we were eating finger foods, that was okay, but where were the napkins? Fingers were getting messy and the boys all talked with their mouths full—this was unacceptable. It took everything I had to not scold or condemn them out loud. Sam, who I had nourished so fully with the etiquette of dining, was following their lead. By the grace of God, I got through dinner without losing my cool. Afterward, I helped Jim clean up the mess. I kept my feelings about the bad table manners and lack of napkins to myself. Thank goodness, the family date was coming to an end. I felt exhausted and ready to go home.

More or less, the day was a success. Even though all the motion and noise wore me out, I grew comfortable with Jim and was extremely impressed with how he handled the boys and life in general. He stayed calm, cool, and casual when I would have been chewing nails, and his poise and graciousness shone through. As I drove home, I thought about all this and the possibilities of marriage and blending a family. I wondered if it could be done. I could see how many challenges could arise, but I loved challenges and slowly began to think I could do it. I had plenty of experience handling kids in school and in church. I imagined the self-contained baseball team, the 24/7 laughter of children, and the comfort and security of being married to such a kind, handsome, Christian man. Was I still thinking?

* * *

Week after week, we took turns visiting each other on the weekends. I was having a ball, and I know he was, too. Jim was very romantic, sending me more love poems. He called me every night, and we began to settle down to seeing each other exclusively. I had tried to date others, but my heart was not in it, and I ultimately took down all my profiles from the matchmaking sites.

During my internet dating adventure, I had met a man who lived in Dallas. He had driven all the way to Colorado City to meet me, and well, I thought I was in love. He was handsome and debonair, and I was convinced he matched exactly what I wanted. He would call from time to time, and every time my heart would jump into a new dimension. In a very sexy voice on the phone, he would say, "Hi, there." I would immediately drop all plans, take Sam to a friend's or my parents' house, and jump on a plane to Dallas to be mesmerized by this man, for maybe six hours!

You see, Mr. Debonair had custody of teenage boys, and they always took precedence over an internet fling. I had planned a trip in August to Mexico, and with one last-ditch effort to keep that relationship going, I invited him to go. Like many other times, he was too busy. Oftentimes, he would have other commitments and could not make the time to see me. Sometimes, I thought he was still married, and Aunt Mollie conveniently kept that thought going in my head, too. So when he declined, I invited Jim to take his place.

Wow! Jim took the bull by the horns and ran with it. He said he would love to go to Mexico, and he even made all the arrangements. He booked our reservations, gave me the itinerary, and all I had to do was show up. What a deal! No one had ever taken care of me like this. He told me we were leaving on Tuesday with a stay-over in Dallas, and we would return on Sunday. We would be staying at an all-inclusive resort in Cancun, and the price was very reasonable. I still felt leery about the triplets, but they weren't going on this trip. I was anxious to see how it would go. We planned to take Sam, so we reserved two rooms. I was curious how Jim and Sam would get along without the interference of the other three boys.

Before the trip, I made all the arrangements to be gone, including canceling piano lessons and getting a substitute for the choir at church. I cleaned Marge and Lucky's house one more time before departure so I could be ready to leave Tuesday morning. Sam and I were all packed and ready to roll when I got a phone call from Jim. He had made a mistake. What? Men who made mistakes like this didn't get a lot of stars on their bonnet. The flight did not leave until Wednesday and he had given me the wrong day.

Since we already had loaded the car with our luggage, Jim suggested Sam and I spend the night at his house. I agreed to come to Lubbock that day. Immediately, I felt guilty about all the arrangements I had made that could have been avoided, but hey, it was not my fault. It was his, and I had learned years ago not to take responsibility for other people's faults. I quickly got over it, threw Sam in the car, and we headed north.

When we arrived at Jim's house, he greeted us with a paper sack over his head. He had a sad face painted on the sack with holes cut out for his eyes. It was pretty cheesy, but cute at the same time. He apologized but didn't seem in the least bit worried about the inconvenience. His eyes were still twinkling, and he had written a love poem the night before. How could I resist?

I had warned him at the beginning that most things that went wrong would be his fault. He grinned and said he could take it. Sure enough, this was the first test, and he was doing a great job. Smooth, calm, charming, poised (eyes sparkling), even in the midst of a big blunder, Jim was doing splendidly.

We visited and all played cards that afternoon, and then we went out to dinner. I will never forget that evening. Jim picked a place that was ideal for kids with coins, while adults could sit and relax. The second blended family get-together turned out to be very relaxing, and Sam was content. After a fun evening out, we returned to Jim's house.

Still, very orderly and clean, the three-bedroom house smelled fresh, and we felt very much at home. Jim gave Sam and I the spare bedroom, because the triplets had all slept in the same room since birth. Try to imagine a small bedroom with three twin beds placed in a very efficient manner. The triplets had a small closet, but there was no room for a dresser. Sam and I slept great in the spare bedroom.

The next day, we enjoyed a somewhat leisurely morning, and then got ready to leave. Our flight left around 1:00 that afternoon, so we did not have a whole lot of time to spare. Just from observation, I was going to enjoy traveling with Jim. He was very organized, neat and tidy, well-dressed, and excited to embark on this somewhat strange adventure. Sam was revved up, and I felt excited as well. This was going to be fun!

We flew into Dallas from Lubbock and took a shuttle to

our hotel. Jim checked us in, and soon we were heading to our room on the eleventh floor. He was being so efficient and accommodating, and I had a hard time accepting all of this. In all my forty-five years, I had never seen such a man. He led us to our hotel room door and inserted the key card. No dice. It didn't work.

"Let me try." When it still failed to unlock, I said, "Is this the right door?"

We appeared to have a faulty card. Jim left us to go get it re-programmed and came back in a jiffy. Re-try. Re-insert. Still, no dice.

I asked again, "Are you sure this is the right door?"

I could tell Jim was getting a little agitated. He went back to the check-in desk and once again left us in the hall with the luggage. When he rounded the corner, he was grinning from ear to ear with that twinkle in his eye. "Wrong room!"

You see, it was his fault again, but he was laughing. Was this guy for real? I was so impressed that he was laughing at himself and we all hooted. It was probably that very moment I realized I had a very special feeling for this amazing gentleman.

* * *

The flight to Cancun the next morning left at 6:00 a.m., so we had to get up at 3:00 a.m. and be back at the airport by 4:00. That did not leave much time for rest. We all got up, and with a little apprehension and anxiety, we got ready, packed, and headed out the door. We were still half-asleep, but eager to get to Cancun.

At the airport, we made our way up to the ticket counter. Reservations? Check. IDs? Check. Since Sam was a minor, the airline agent asked if his father had given me permission to let Sam leave the country. Very calmly, I told her his father was deceased. Then, she informed me she needed a death certificate. *Do what?*

I began to shake. Jim asked calmly if I had one and I did, but it was at home. What were we going to do? The agent said it needed to be certified and she needed it by 5:00 a.m. We got out of line and retreated to the side to think about our options. There were not very many, and I was panicking. Either we cancel the trip to Mexico altogether or we call my other sister in Arlington and ask if she could come get Sam. Caye was a wonderful aunt. She had a daughter about a year older than Sam, and they had spent several summer weeks together. Even if we decided to go on to Mexico and leave Sam with Caye, we did not know if it would be convenient for her to keep him for four days. This had never even been discussed because, from day one, Sam was going with us.

I became an emotional wreck. Sam started to cry and I wasn't far behind.

Jim calmly bent down to Sam, took his shoulders in his hands and said, "It is going to be okay. We are going to figure this out." Then he rose and took my shoulders in his hands. "Let's think about this. Is there anyone in Colorado City who could go to your house, get the death certificate and fax it here?"

I blinked and looked in his face. My mind began to churn and we were soon on the same page. In my absence, my Methodist preacher's daughter was to feed our dog and goldfish, and she had a key to the house. If I could get the preacher to get up, get the key from his daughter and go to my house, I could give him the whereabouts of the death certificate, and he could take it to the church office to get it faxed. Was this asking too much? It was 4:00 in the morning! Jim quickly excused himself to the ticket counter to ask if they would accept a certified fax of the certificate. They would!

Quickly, he led me to the pay phones and handed me his credit card. "You are going to have to hurry, Lynette." He was sure that Monte, our pastor, would do it because Jim had met him during that very first visit to Colorado City and they had visited while I was tied up with children. Jim knew if I told him what the deal was, he would help. Luckily, because of my position at the church, I had the pastor's phone number memorized. After four rings, he answered.

I explained the circumstances and he said he would do it. He called me when he got to my house, and I led him to the filing cabinet that contained the death certificate. He told me he was heading to the church and would call me when he got it faxed. That way, we could check with the ticket agent to make sure she received it before Monte went back to bed. I told him I owed him one, and he certainly did not argue. Again, he said he would call me back.

Minutes seemed like hours, but Monte finally called, and we got authorization from the ticket agent that the faxed death certificate was there. I called Monte back, told him how grateful we were, and gave him permission to go home and go back to bed.

We hurriedly made our way to the security gates. It was almost 6:00 a.m. and we were on our way. Jim was my hero! But what about losing his way to Colorado City to meet me for the very first time? What about getting the dates wrong for the trip? What about trying to get into the wrong hotel room? These events had bothered me at the time, but I erased them… for the time being.

The vacation in Cancun was close to perfect. The three of us played together in the beautiful turquoise waters of the Caribbean, went on long beach walks, and did plenty of shell hunting. We built sand castles and tried our hand at shuffleboard.

The second evening, Sam was feeling less than normal. At dinnertime, he just wanted to crawl in bed. Jim understood. He knelt down close to Sam, looked him in the eye, and gently said, "Would it be okay if I took your mom out to dinner?" When Jim offered to order room service, Sam was puzzled. He was probably thinking, *What is room service?* Never in our meager lives had I ever splurged on room service.

Jim's eyes gleamed at me, and then he began to explain room service to my son.

Sam's eyes lit up, but he was bewildered. He asked Jim, "You mean we can actually order anything we want and get it delivered here?"

Jim read the menu out loud, and Sam decided on a hot dog with French fries (a staple at our house). I could see that Jim and Sam were beginning to bond.

After his dinner arrived (of course, Mexican style), Jim set him up with a movie for kids, and Sam was eager for us to leave so he could enjoy these luxuries, which were not customary at home. Since the resort was all-inclusive, the restaurant was not far from our room. I felt safe and secure with the arrangement, so Jim and I ventured out for a romantic dinner all to ourselves. I was in Heaven!

As we walked to the restaurant, he put his right hand on the small of my back, and I bristled at first. Since Sam's dad had died, I had not felt anything like this. I took a deep breath and relaxed. *What's the worst that could happen?* I was not going to fall in love with this man.

As we entered the restaurant, the host pulled out my chair, and we took our seats. We surveyed the menu, but Jim had done his research. He suggested the chef's choice: grilled scallops with broccoli spears. It was indescribable. Not only was the food unforgettable, the evening was perfect. Jim showed plenty of interest in me. Every question he asked was followed by a pause and a sense of curiosity. It seemed as though when I spoke, every answer was acceptable. I also had questions for him, and he answered them honestly and without precipitation. It was all very refreshing.

We talked about the triplets and their life of switching weekly from Mom's house to Dad's house. We discussed Sam and the loss of his father, about Derek, my older son, and about Josh and Jon, Jim's older sons who I had not yet met. Somehow, we were finding common ground and figuring out a plan of how this might work. The conversation mesmerized and dazzled me. Could this union really work?

As dinner ended, we decided to check on Sam. He was fast asleep, so we headed toward the beach for a stroll. The night was clear, fresh, moonstruck, and glorious. We walked barefoot in the sand, holding hands. Several times we stopped along the way, held each other and kissed gently. I was beginning not to think so clearly.

During the period of being in the dating scene, I had found that most prospects were not really interested in my life, but exactly what I could bring to the table. Usually, the conversation was all about them until it turned to how I could make their life better. With Jim, it was all about how he could make my life better for me and Sam. It was very different, and a little disconcerting. Was this for real? Could Jim actually be my Prince Charming, the man of my dreams?

How easily I could forget about the triplets and the chaos back home in Texas. It was surprising how quickly I could imagine leaving all the hard work in Colorado City and starting a new life with Jim in Lubbock. The beautiful Mexican resort, the sea breeze, turquoise water, and sunshine were having an effect on me, and I had the faint idea that maybe I was losing my ability to think.

Four

Cody, Caleb, and Cooper were the triplets' names. Sam and I called them "The Three C's." They were not identical, thank goodness! I had always wondered how parents distinguished identical twins from each other, much less triplets. Their parents had decided to have another child later in life and had needed some extra help with making that happen. Well into their forties, they had trouble reproducing. Even though they only wanted one baby, five fertile eggs were inserted (basic procedure) and three took hold. When the doctor told the proud parents they could choose to keep one, they chose the alternative. Their mother was going to try to carry all three boys to full term, and she almost succeeded. The boys ended up coming a little premature. Caleb and Cooper were fine and healthy, but Cody was born with a muscular disorder. He would be fine, but his physical development would be somewhat slower than his brothers.

From the time the triplets were about three, the parents had divorced, so the boys spent one week with their mother, then one week with their dad. They switched back and forth between homes every week. They had been doing this for quite some time, and it seemed to be working. If Jim and I were to marry, the arrangement was good for me because I would have every other week to regroup and rest. I could gradually get used to the idea of being a stepmom. Wait a minute! Jim had not even asked me to marry him, so why was I thinking about marriage?

We continued to date and see each other on weekends, and I totally enjoyed the time with Jim, with and without the triplets. I could see that the triplets were a lot of work, but they would continue to be Jim's responsibility when they lived with him. I had my boys to worry about.

One weekend, Jim was at my home in Colorado City. Sam was spending the night with his best friend and the triplets were with their mom, so we were alone. We were having a candlelight dinner (yes, I am a romantic), so I took the quiet opportunity to ask Jim if having one more boy would bother him. I will never forget his reply. He lifted one eyebrow and grinned as he said, "If I already have three living at home, one more is not going to make any difference." He took my hand and kissed it. He was actually worried about me, because he knew having one was very different from having four. He was not so blind.

One evening we were chatting, and Jim asked if I would consider marrying him. I thought he was teasing and I jokingly responded, "Not sure. Would I have to work?"

I was exhausted from teaching school and piano lessons, cleaning houses, and being the music minister and Kids' Club director at church.

He said, "You won't have to work unless you want to."

What? A permanent vacation? He looked me square in the eye, told me he just wanted to take care of me, and at that moment, I started taking him seriously. The fact that someone wanted to take care of me suddenly seemed as close to Heaven as I had ever been. From that point on, we started making plans to be married, but you see, he had not actually proposed…yet. I guess he was still thinking, too.

Jim made plans for us to go to Santa Fe in October to the balloon festival without any children. Once again, he handled all the arrangements and all I had to do was show up. This man was a keeper!

When we landed in Albuquerque, he had rented a yellow convertible Mustang to drive to Santa Fe. We stayed at a very romantic hotel, and on Saturday afternoon as we strolled through the plaza, he produced the most beautiful ring I had ever seen and proposed. In a way, I knew it was coming, but I was still speechless.

Eventually, I found my voice and told him, "Yes!" I could not believe I was finally getting married! It seemed too good to be true.

We began talking about dates and thought it would be best to wait until the next summer. That would give us more time to get to know each other. Sam could get used to the idea and we would not have to move him during the school year. That idea did not stick. We were both getting tired of the weekend drive (200 miles round trip), and we were adults. After all, we had made a decision, we knew we wanted to spend the rest of our lives together, and we could not justify waiting. Sam would adjust. Besides, he already liked the idea of having three instant, permanent playmates. A little affirmation from Aunt Mollie was all it took. When she said, "Why wait?" we decided to take the plunge.

We planned the wedding for January 4, 2003, but the more I thought about it, the more sense it made to marry before Christmas. That way, we could spend Christmas together and Jim would be able to claim us as dependents on his taxes. He agreed. We had to get moving because the date we set was December 21, 2002, and it was already late October.

I put my house up for sale and had a contract on it within a week. Unbelievable! Houses do not sell quickly in Colorado City, and I did not have to come down on the price. All the buyers wanted were some repairs done in the basement. I called a good friend, got that scheduled, and things started clicking. Inspections were done, surveys made, and it looked like I would be moving to Lubbock very quickly.

* * *

I decided to have a garage sale to decrease the mass to move, and Jim said he would help. It was his weekend to have the boys and I felt a little concerned, but Jim was so easy and confident. He said it would be fine, he would take care of them, and he would be able to help me, too. Sam's best friend's mom planned to bring some stuff to add to the merchandise, so I would have her help, as well. I was not so sure about having five children under the age of eight at a garage sale, but my mom and sister were coming from Abilene and that made the ratio of adults to children 1:1. Surely, it would be okay.

The day went smoother than expected. Customers came in droves and my friend, Penny, was very efficient. Jim managed to help load the heavy items as they sold, and tended to the boys the rest of the time. My mom and sister arrived about 11:00 and helped serve lunch, which consisted of a huge pot of taco soup to have with chips and drinks. The adults helped the children with their plates, and Jim corralled the children around the kitchen table. Since I stayed mostly in the garage, I was not aware of what actually happened in the kitchen or how much food they consumed. I had a feeling that soup was not common for the triplets, so they probably survived on chips and cookies.

Late in the afternoon when we had a little time to look at the merchandise left for sale, I noticed the toy aisle was almost empty. Had we actually sold that many toys and games? No, but yes! As Jim was loading up his van to take the triplets back to Lubbock, I saw the back end was packed full of Sam's old pastimes. At that point I found out just how much of an ole softie Jim really was. Through the course of the day, I had noticed the boys' involvement with the tossed aside toys, but it never occurred to me they were carting them to the van, and Jim was paying the asking price. Realistically, we did not get rid of the toys; we merely transported them to a different location.

As the day ended and Jim's van pulled out of the driveway, a lump caught in my throat. Sam also seemed sad to watch his future family leave. He was thrilled with the idea of blending families and having a father. Since the three C's called Jim

"Dad," it seemed very natural for Sam to call him the same. Geez, I was even starting to call him "Dad" myself!

One of the things that most attracted me to Jim was the fact that he was a Christian and a devout Methodist. During my ventures into internet dating, Christianity was an essential prerequisite for any potential match. The denomination wasn't that important, but it was icing on the cake that Jim was also a member of the Methodist Church. You see? He was perfect for me, in many ways. Jim might have been busy doing other things on Sundays, but he never failed to take those boys to church. He always attended the early service and took them to Sunday school. Then he either headed home or dropped them off at their mother's, depending on whose week it was to keep them.

I happened to be in Lubbock one Sunday when Sam had stayed in Colorado City with a friend, and it was the boys' weekend to stay with their mom. Jim did not want me go with him to pick them up for church, so he had to leave early to have enough time to get them, and then come back to the house to get me. I was ready when they got back. We were going to stop and get some donuts before heading to church, so I hurriedly jumped in the van and we took off.

We got to the church and filed the little boys into the pew. I had not been to church with Jim since we started dating, since I had my responsibilities back home, but I had found a substitute and decided to treat myself to attending church with my future husband. There were just a handful of people there, and soon I could see why Jim chose to take the boys to this small intimate service. What a fiasco!

I wasn't sure if the triplets were high on sugar from donuts or displaying normal behavior, but they became the busiest little boys I had ever been around. They were everywhere—climbing over the pews, climbing under the pews, hunting for pencils placed in the slots for guests' registration, and drawing on everything in sight. The church had provided children's kits for the younger attendees, but there was just a sprinkling of supplies compared to what was needed to keep this little group quiet and occupied.

Poor Jim. No, poor *me*! He would bend and get one boy up off the floor and calmly sit him in his seat. No sooner than he was through settling the first boy, he was grabbing another to keep him from walking out in the aisle. Then there was the one who thought it would be great fun to climb over the back of the pew and land in the lap of the poor soul sitting behind us.

I was a wreck, in disbelief that three little boys could be so active and in continuous motion for the full forty-five minutes. I didn't hear one thing that went on during that service. Watching them made me exhausted, and these were not even my children! By mid-morning, I felt like I'd done a full day's work.

After the service ended, thankfully, we led the boys out of the sanctuary and Jim took them to their Sunday school class. While their teacher greeted them and showed them to their places, I felt a compassion for her. They were not going to stay in their seats.

Jim and I did not stick around to watch. We headed toward the Sunday school class that he had been attending, and he introduced me to the small group. That was when I met Dennie and Dave Treat, a couple about our age. Dave was a retired pastor. Retired? Yes, I thought he was a little too young to be retired, but what did I know? Anyway, if he were still preaching, he would not have time to teach a Sunday school class. Also, I had learned it was very hard to get close to a church pastor unless you were either staff or an elder. This was great! Dave could be my friend/pastor. It's always nice to have a direct line to Heaven if you need a little spiritual help. I expected I might need more than just a little venturing into this new experience. We did not get to visit with Dennie and Dave much that Sunday, but the introduction officially started our friendship. I had some new acquaintances in the new church and I liked them. Coming to Jim's church felt good.

After Sunday school, he rounded up the boys and we headed home. We fed them their usual lunch of finger foods—chicken nuggets and tater tots—and then Jim took them back to their mom's house. While left alone with time to think, I replayed the morning in my head and pondered about the Three C's' behavior in church. When Jim got home, I asked him if he had ever thought about sitting the boys down and telling them what they could and could not do in church, and if he had ever talked about expectations. Nope. No wonder they were everywhere but sitting their bottoms in the pews. They had never been taught how to behave in church.

What else had they not been taught?

My heart was filled with love for this man, but did I really know what I was getting into? No, and I did not care. I wanted to be married to Jim, and my sister and aunt had said, "You can handle it." I was determined that, no matter what, I would handle it. I wanted to live in Lubbock, become a member of the United Methodist Church with Jim, and for our families to blend into one big happy family. I wanted Sam to have a father and for Jim to be his father.

* * *

Sam and I began to talk about the move to Lubbock and starting a new school. We all knew it would be tough, but Sam was a trooper, and super eager to start his new life. School in Colorado City let out the whole week of Thanksgiving, but the Lubbock schools stayed in session Monday and Tuesday before Thanksgiving Day. We decided to move Sam to Lubbock the weekend before Thanksgiving.

On Friday, Jim and Derek drove down from Lubbock to Colorado City in Derek's truck to help with the move. We loaded up Sam's bed and dresser, packed his clothes and belongings, and threw in his roller blades and bicycle. To me, it was like sending a son off to college. Of course, I would be 100 miles away, but it still felt strange. I would stay with Sam and Jim until we left to be with my family for Thanksgiving, but I was still the one being left behind. I had to keep telling myself to get over it. I would only be in Colorado City by myself for a few more weeks. Then Jim and I would be married, and we would all be together.

Just a few more weeks…

After church on Sunday, we spent all day putting Sam's room together. We moved furniture around, hung pictures, placed bookshelves and knickknacks, and finally by dinner, we were through. His room looked awesome and he was excited. He couldn't wait to show the triplets, and asked, "Mom, when will they get here?"

They were scheduled to arrive at six that evening. It was Jim's week to have the Three C's, and I would experience first-hand the process of getting four little boys dressed, fed, and off to school the next day. I was in for a realization that should have caused me to run screaming out the front door.

When the triplets finally arrived, Sam proudly showed them his room. They thought it was the coolest thing they had ever seen. Since birth, they had shared the same room, and now saw what it was like for someone to have their own room. They were envious of Sam and his space, but they all handled it well. The boys felt so happy that he had moved in, they didn't seem to realize that having his own room was somewhat considered to be "special treatment."

* * *

In addition to being the Director of the Student Mediation Center at Tech, Jim also worked as a magistrate for the city. When scheduled to magistrate, Jim would get up at 4:00 a.m. and leave the house at 4:30 a.m. to perform his duties. He usually returned by 6:00 a.m., and of course, the city court never scheduled him to magistrate when the triplets were staying at his house. The court needed a substitute for Monday morning, and since Jim knew I would be at his house, he agreed to go.

I heard him come home and I got up that morning to greet him. I fixed a pot of coffee and we sat quietly in the kitchen, sipping coffee and talking about the events to come. Neither of us was really thinking; we were starry-eyed and in love. Extremely happy, we relished in our hopes for the future. We intended to have a good life and grow old together. Isn't that what every couple believes when they decide to get married?

Jim finished his cup of coffee and told me it was time to get the boys up and ready for school. I asked him if he needed help and he politely said, "No, thanks. I've got this."

I knew how long it took Sam to get ready, so I was going to let him sleep a little longer. Sipping my coffee, I waited and watched.

Jim disappeared into the triplets' room. In a few seconds he came out with Cody. He walked into the living room, set him on the couch (immediately Cody laid back down; Jim set him back up), and then Jim turned on the television. He disappeared back into their room and reappeared with Caleb. He sat Caleb on the couch next to Cody. Same thing happened with Cooper. Finally, Jim had them all sitting on the couch like three little monkeys, half asleep, but glued to the television, because Barney, the dancing-singing purple dinosaur, held the triplets spellbound.

Now, I understood why the entertainment center in the living room was not used to house the television or stereo. It provided open, easy-to-get-to shelving for the boys' clothes, underwear, and shoes. Jim picked out enough clothes to dress one child and began to take Cody's pajamas off. He then proceeded to dress Cody, each piece separately down to the socks and shoes. In turn, Jim dressed each boy the same way until fully clothed. Not once did any of them take their eyes off the television. The triplets didn't know what they had on, but they had not missed one dance step of Barney's.

Jim neatly folded all of their pajamas and put them in their respective places on the entertainment center. I was amazed. No, shocked. I could not believe that six-year-old first graders were not dressing themselves. Had they never been taught, or had they never even had the desire to learn? I had seen more than I wanted to see.

At the next event, breakfast, Jim brought three highchairs into the kitchen area. One by one, he put sleepy little boys into their highchairs and snapped on the trays.

Highchairs for six-year-olds! What is this man thinking?

Jim started getting boxes out of the freezer: pop tarts, cinnamon sticks, sausage biscuits, and pancakes rolled around sausages. I got Sam up, so he could join the other boys. Sam loved the choices! Never before had he seen such a variety of breakfast foods. This was all a big mystery to my son because all we ever had was toast, cereal, bacon, or oatmeal. I'm sure he thought he had woken up in a different world.

After breakfast, Jim herded the boys to the bathroom. I also learned that Jim was putting toothpaste on their toothbrushes and individually brushing their teeth, one by one. This was not normal! Jim did everything for the boys and they did nothing for themselves. No wonder he was exhausted by the time Sunday rolled around and they went back to their mom's. For me to remain sane living in this household, things would to have to change; but I needed to be careful. My "take control, drill sergeant" attitude would come in handy, but would it overwhelm everyone? Yes, even me.

Finally, Jim took the boys to school. No matter who had the boys, the other parent would meet them at the school at 7:30 to say good morning and best wishes for a great day. That really impressed me. Sam and I would leave a little later because school didn't start until 8:00 and there was no rush. We had to do a little paperwork in the office before we would be shown to his class.

Despite Sam's excitement, he felt very nervous about starting school. I never knew an eight-year-old boy could be so worried about the way he looked. Suddenly, his pants were too short and his shoes looked like skis. After many, many compliments, I coerced him to get in the car and we headed to school.

Jim met us in the office after he got through with his boys. It was so nice to have him there for support. Of course, he knew all the staff, so introductions were easy and comfortable. We finished the paperwork, then one of the counselors led all of us to Sam's room. I could see in Sam's face that he was an emotional wreck. His eyes said, "Get me out of here! I don't want to stay!"

We met his teacher. I could tell she was not too keen on getting a brand new student at the end of the semester. I could see the fear on Sam's face; I felt it, too. I gave him a hug and he clung to me like glue. Jim bent down and told him he understood. He took Sam from my arms and told him how proud he was of him. Jim gave my son a massive hug and assured him that everything would be okay, we would see him this afternoon.

I wanted to stay and make sure Sam was safe.

Jim looked at me and smiled. "I promise, it will be okay."

I tried to believe him, but was still cautious. I gave Sam another hug and promised I'd be back. Jim led me out into the hallway, but my heart stayed in that classroom with Sam.

* * *

A week or two before I knew we would register Sam for school, I had asked Jim for a special favor. Since Sam's father was deceased, and since I was conveniently marrying an attorney, I asked if we could get Sam's name changed to Albright. I had already spoken to Sam about it and he was on board. Not only was he cool with the fact that he would have the same last name as everyone else, I explained he might be first in line with the last name of Albright.

Jim thought the name change was a wonderful idea and proceeded to the courthouse. When he took the papers to the judge, she asked, "Jim, are you nuts?"

He just grinned and said, "No, but Lynette is."

You see, the judge knew his situation and really thought Jim was taking on more responsibility than he should. It was apparent she cared about him. Not long after, I learned that his close friends felt concerned as well. Jim was very well liked and respected. I could see that I would have to find a slot in his life that hopefully would be accepted by his friends and relatives.

When I went to get Sam from school that afternoon, it was just as I'd expected. He was NOT going back. He wanted to move back to Colorado City and into that 1940s house on 10th Street. He didn't like being the new kid at school. Everyone had stared at Sam all day, and no one made him feel welcome. Only one teacher offered him kindness.

Have any of you heard that motto that buzzes around teachers: "Make a difference"? Well, this one teacher made

Sam feel special. If it hadn't been for her, I don't think he would have ever survived. Third graders changed classes some, and she was his math teacher. Thank God for those teachers who are determined to make a difference.

Somehow, we got through Monday and Tuesday. Wednesday, we left the Albright house to head to Abilene. I couldn't wait to visit with Mom and Carole to get their feelings over the garage sale ordeal. Of course, I knew that marriage to Jim had to be my decision, but our family was very close, and it always seemed like a good idea to get their approval. Was it a good idea? No, it was imperative!

Everyone loved Jim. Carole thought the Three C's were precious. At the garage sale she, too, had been very impressed with how well Jim handled the boys. She said she would have been screaming, but Jim always spoke to them with a calm, low voice.

Carole said, "Go for it!"

All my mom could say was, "The young is for the young," and sadly shook her head. I think she was a little overwhelmed and also wondering if I knew what I was getting into. Truth was, I didn't have a clue, but I knew I wanted this man as my husband. Sam didn't know what he was getting into either, but he knew he wanted a dad and a ready-made family. With all my heart, I hoped that we could be a happy, blended family. I was certain that we would succeed, because God was on our side. So far, there had been no huge obstacles to keep us from moving forward. Despite the fact that becoming a stepmom was going to take a whole lot of work and patience, those three little red flags had found a place in my heart.

Five

Jim took a personal day from work that Monday after Thanksgiving, and we headed off to get some plans finalized for the wedding. Our first appointment was with the wedding counselor at the church. Surprise! She just happened to be Dennie Treat, the lady I met in Sunday school, the retired preacher's wife. She was terrific. I will never forget the moment when she asked us if we were going to need a rehearsal the evening before the wedding. Jim was so cute when he told her he thought we had both been married enough times before, and we knew how to do it without a rehearsal.

I had no idea how long it would really take, but Jim and I spent a full three hours with her. Whew! I knew we had to make many decisions concerning the church and use of their equipment and facilities, but I believe Jim was a little overwhelmed. I really put him through the ringer that day.

From there, we headed to the florist. After asking the consultant several questions and getting prices on some floral arrangements, I did not feel comfortable. We headed to another florist and went through the same motions. The second florist hit a homerun. I liked their suggestions, and they agreed to send me a formal proposal. Only later did I realize that I would have to cut the flowers to about half of the price. Oh, brother! I had forgotten weddings were so expensive.

From there, we went to the bakery and looked at all kinds of designs, colors, shapes and forms. We talked about flavors and tried to decide if we wanted a groom's cake, too, or just the traditional wedding cake. When we started thinking about the full scope of the price of a wedding, we decided to check out the bakery at the local grocery store. Bingo! Another homerun. We would just have the one wedding cake, plain vanilla, and at half the cost of a specialized bakery cake. We were making progress.

Jim had a beautiful linen suit he would wear to be married in, but we stopped at a men's clothing store and picked out a new shirt and beautiful tie. We didn't squabble about the price, because I knew when it came time to pick out my dress, I wasn't going to worry about the cost too much. I wanted our wedding attire to be perfect, and I was prepared to pay the price. Jim gave the man his credit card, then we went on our way again.

One more stop and we could go home. But wait! I looked at Jim and he looked ragged. And his eyes had lost their sparkle. Instead of making "one more stop," we headed for the liquor store so he could get some bourbon. After what I'd drug him through and all the negotiations with consultants, I'm sure he wanted a drink. I did, too, but I am a recovered alcoholic and having a drink with Jim would not be a good idea.

Being an alcoholic is just another paradox of this whole story. At the time I met Jim, I had achieved about nine years of sobriety, but had almost totally quit going to meetings. I hadn't been drinking, but some might question the quality of my sobriety. Sometimes, alcoholics can be dry without truly being sober. Often, when we get off track and don't follow the twelve steps in our daily living, we begin to practice "stinking thinking." *Could I be there and not know it?* I wondered. *Heaven forbid! I better find some AA meetings in Lubbock.*

After we stopped at the store and picked up Sam, it was time for me to head back to Colorado City. Jim assured me that he and the four boys would be fine. Sam looked a little leery, but I knew he would be okay. He felt very comfortable with Jim and they had a good relationship going. We had arrangements in place for after school care, and there was no need for me to worry. Yeah, right! What mother wouldn't worry? I had a lot of confidence in Jim, but I also knew that he would never be as good of a dad to my son as I was a mother. Enough said.

*　*　*

Since I was busy with lessons, rehearsals, and choir practice, the week flew by and I could head back to Lubbock. I quit teaching, which enabled me to leave on Thursday after piano lessons. The triplets' mom was going out of town for the weekend, so Jim would get the triplets Friday after school instead of the usual Sunday evening.

I had a hard time trying to decide what to feed the boys that they might like. They had not been forced to eat any vegetables or fruit. During the time that Jim and I had dated, most of the time at least one of them was sick. I was convinced that their diet had a great deal to do with their poor health. I made it my mission to get this family healthy. You see, if the boys were sick, they would be at home with me when they could be at school. Jim had left me at home all day so I could follow up with the wedding plans, unload and unpack one more haul from Colorado City, go to the grocery store to get stocked for the weekend, and cook dinner. Sam loves my stew, so I chose to serve a simple stew with potatoes, tomatoes, and beef. It made the kitchen smell good, and with Sam's support, it was sure to be a hit. I had dinner all ready when Jim and the boys walked in the door.

"Hey!"

"Hello!"

"How are you?"

"How was school?"

"How was your day?"

Then Cooper blurted out that dreaded question, "What's for dinner?"

Everyone fell quiet. I just stood there, searching for the words that wouldn't sabotage my plan. I knew "stew" wasn't the most appetizing choice. All of their little faces were glued on mine as I struggled to find the right thing to say. "It's soup! We're having soup for dinner."

They all looked bewildered, even Sam. He had never had homemade "soup" for dinner. He would have been jumping for joy for "stew."

Again, inquisitive Cooper asked, "What kind of soup?"

Geez! I didn't have a clue what to say. Good soup? Hot soup? Yummy soup?

While I was still struggling, Cooper called out, "Is it the kind you eat with crackers?"

He was my hero! I was saved. Relieved, I said, "Yes, it's the kind you eat with crackers."

This was going to work. My hopes were quickly dashed when he cried out, "I don't like that kind of soup!"

I was still trying to show my good side. Instead of getting in his face and yelling, "You don't know because you've never tried it!" I calmly said, "Well, you don't have to eat crackers with this soup. Go wash your hands and come back and sit down, please."

Jim kissed me and said, "It smells wonderful."

I was so in love with this man. He was going to save me when all seemed hopeless. As soon as Sam found out it was really *stew*, he talked it up just as fast as he could. He told the younger boys it was awesome and if they'd just try it, they'd like it. What would I do without him? In spite of his efforts, I had a gut feeling dinner was going to be a disaster.

Sure enough, it was. The boys were rude, wouldn't try it, hurt my feelings, and all while Sam tried with all his might to build a bridge. Jim was not a lot of help, because he had never had trouble getting the boys to eat chicken nuggets or hot dogs. I was too new at this stepmother thing to try to force some behavior, so needless to say, all the boys ate were crackers. We had cornbread, too, but of course they didn't know what that yellow stuff was either, and they were bound and determined not to eat anything new. I had a long row to hoe ahead of me.

I learned a lot about the boys through that disastrous dinner. Cooper had a strong personality and was not afraid to ask questions. He kept asking if he could have a hot dog or nuggets, and I kept saying, "That is not what we are having for dinner tonight."

Then, he would just stare at me defiantly. Cooper was also the biggest of the three boys and a voracious eater, observed by the number of crackers he ate! Since he seemed to be the leader of the pack, in spite of Sam, I figured if I could win Cooper over with some normal food, I might have a chance with the others. Caleb and Cody were mostly quiet, but I could tell they were not going to eat one bite of that "soup you eat with crackers!"

After dinner, the boys played outside. Jim's house had a nice back yard, and since it was fall, the evenings were fairly nice. Jim and I stayed inside and caught each other up on the week's events. Things were going to get a little hectic as the date of the wedding was getting closer, and with three weeks to go, it was time to get the invitations out. I insisted he get his list together, because we were planning a trip to Aunt Mollie's the next weekend to get her final approval. She had never met Jim, and she had graciously offered to help me address and get the invitations in the mail.

The rest of the weekend was pretty uneventful (if you can call it that with four boys undertow), except for the eating situation. I had bought lots of fruits and vegetables, and as far as the boys were concerned, these foods were from outer space. Saturday night I fixed chicken fried steak fingers, mashed potatoes, gravy, and green beans.

As I was putting the green beans on their plates, Cooper, my hero, said, "What's that?"

Exasperated, I replied, "Green Beans! Hasn't your mother ever fixed you vegetables?"

I will never forget what he said, "No…she doesn't know what they are!"

Caleb was angelic and very much a people pleaser. After the prayer, I showed everyone how to hold a fork, because they didn't even know their purpose. Caleb got the fork held right, but Cooper and Cody were struggling.

I didn't make a fuss about it; that would come later. I said, "Now, stab a green bean with it, lift it up, and put it in your mouth, please."

Caleb reluctantly put his in his mouth. He didn't chew. He looked at me and I smiled and nodded in approval. He did not smile back. Cooper and Cody still held theirs in mid-air. Seconds later, Caleb gagged and spit his out in his plate.

Cooper yelled, "No way am I eating that!"

Cody just put his fork down and shook his head.

Sam said, "Come on guys, these are good! Just try them."

No bueno.

Since they were used to finger foods, I tried the steak fingers. I said, "Okay, try these. You do not have to use a fork. You can use your fingers. Pick up one of these and take a bite. They are just like chicken nuggets but longer and tastier." I picked up one of mine and demonstrated. I even showed them how they could put ketchup, gravy, or both on them.

Cooper said, "What is ketchup?"

Seriously? I guess the parents were trying to keep things simple and cleaner, so no ketchup was ever offered. Sam told them ketchup was great and kept eating. He tried to encourage them to try it, but they didn't trust him. Jim was tasting everything and telling the boys it was good. Caleb held a steak finger in his hand, but didn't take a bite. Cooper and Caleb refused to even pick one up.

Next were the mashed potatoes. Homemade mashed potatoes, at that—a lot of effort on my part. I tried to explain to them that they were the same as French fries but mashed up.

Again, Cooper said very strongly, "These are *not* French fries!"

"They are better than French fries," I said, "because you do not have to chew them so much. They just slide down your throat. Pick up your spoon and get a little bit on the tip of the spoon to try."

They all stared at me and didn't move.

I got up from the table and went to Cody first. I stood behind him and pointed to his spoon. "This is your spoon, Cody. Pick it up, please."

He looked at his dad and Jim nodded. Cody picked it up.

"Good," I encouraged him, "now, scoop up a little."

He picked up a piece of mashed potato the size of a pea.

"Really? I don't think so." I cradled his hand in mine and picked up a little more. Not even a mouthful. "Put it in your mouth, please."

Sam said, "Come on, Cody. They are good!"

Cooper and Caleb were watching intently.

I guided Cody's hand to his mouth but he wouldn't open it.

"Open your mouth, please."

He did, and we put the spooned potatoes in his mouth.

Success! Well, not really. I focused on Caleb and Cooper, and told them how brave Cody was. "He tried it! He liked it! You should try it, too!"

Sam was showing them how good everything was, and I got Caleb and Cooper to try the mashed potatoes, too. Caleb almost gagged again, so he ate them very slowly. They were full of salt and butter so Cooper ate them, too.

In a minute, I noticed Cody was gone from the table. I asked Jim, "What happened to Cody?"

"He needed to go to the bathroom."

Later, I learned that Cody kept excusing himself to the bathroom so he could spit out what he had in his mouth into the toilet.

I had noticed before that a lot of food found its way into the garbage disposal at the Albright household. Even though the boys were only six, Jim filled their plates like they were teenagers. One time, he had told me that while they were with him for the week, they went through four gallons of milk. I was shocked. Then I observed Jim filling each boy's glass full and at the end of the meal, him pouring half of each glass down the sink. The more time I spent with this family, the more I could see changes needed to be made.

* * *

When Sunday morning rolled around, I was determined to enjoy the church service a bit more than the first Sunday I went with Jim and the boys. We were going to the early service again, but this time, before we left, I sat them all down on the couch and told them what was not acceptable to do during the service. I explained carefully and sternly that their bottoms were to stay glued to the pew at all times. They were not to crawl around, over, or under the pews. They were to sit quietly with their children's packets and stay contained. Talking was not allowed. This was God's time, not theirs.

Cooper stared at me defiantly. Cody would not look at me. Caleb said, "Yes, Mom."

What? He called me Mom? My heart melted.

The experience at church that day was better, but much improvement was going to be needed. Constantly, I had to remind the Three C's to sit down. They learned quickly that if they were going to get up, the only thing that would work was if they wanted to sit in their daddy's lap or somewhere different. Then, it was like a fruit basket turnover. They constantly changed places and took turns sitting in Daddy's lap. I was ready to pull out my hair. What was I thinking? Could this really turn into something I could manage? Or something I wanted to manage?

Lunch was the same challenge, but I was determined to "make a difference." I offered more vegetables but encouraged Jim to put less on their plates. Also, I suggested he pour only half a glass of milk for each boy, including Sam. I knew they wouldn't starve, because they were going to their mother's for the next week. We made each boy try one bite of everything, only to have two of them spit it out and the other one to throw up on his plate.

It was going to be okay. I had faith that God had put me where I needed to be. Also, it was almost time for everyone to go home, and I had a week to forget about food and church issues.

* * *

The next week was busier than usual. I put together the final touches for the Christmas program at my church in Colorado City and the recital for my piano students. I also frantically tried to pack during my spare time. Friday, Jim planned to take off early from work, pick up Sam from school, and head to Colorado City. From there, Sam, Jim, and I had plans to drive to Austin to visit my aunt and uncle for the weekend. I had told Jim it was an easy drive from Colorado City to Austin, and we would get there before 10:00 p.m.

I had taken the trip more than a dozen times and knew the road like the back of my hand. Jim drove. Everything seemed fine until we got to the hill country and the two lane roads; then it began to rain. Soon we were driving through a terrible downpour. Jim grew nervous as he steered the car along the unfamiliar, winding roads. That, along with the blinding rain was almost too much. I called Aunt Mollie to say we were on the way, but we'd be late. I could tell she was worried, too. We didn't pull into her driveway until almost midnight. We unloaded and settled in for the night since we were all exhausted and knew we had all day Saturday to get acquainted and get the invitations addressed.

The next morning Aunt Mollie prepared a beautiful spread for breakfast, and we all sat down in the comfortable breakfast area. Uncle Dee offered a beautiful blessing, as usual, and then the questioning began. Every time I had shared a relationship with Uncle Dee, he would always ask, "Is he single and does he have a job?"

This time, I had already answered, "He has been divorced for three years, and he is an attorney." I conveniently forgot to mention he had five sons.

Uncle Dee asked Jim all kinds of questions about his ex-wives, sons, and the triplets. Through this interrogation, I learned that Jim's first wife had a daughter that Jim had been her stepfather for a while. It really didn't bother me, because I figured she would probably never be in the picture. For every question Uncle Dee asked, Jim had a splendid answer. He was unbelievable. He answered every question honestly, and with that twinkle in his eyes. He was not intimidated at all, and my aunt and uncle became very impressed.

The day was wonderful. Uncle Dee and Jim bonded while Aunt Mollie and I worked on the invitations. Uncle Dee took Jim on a tour of the country cub, the swimming pool, the golf course, and the stocked bar at home. I knew Jim loved bourbon, so I feared this might be a mistake. That evening, he got to feeling good, but he was a complete gentleman and a pleasure to be with.

Soon, the weekend was over and the mission accomplished. We had gotten the invitations ready to be mailed and Jim had taken time to visit with Aunt Mollie and Uncle Dee individually. I think they were both pleased with my prospect of a new husband. I had made some pretty poor choices before, but this time it looked like I had a winner. Aunt Mollie pulled me aside to tell me how excited Jim was to get married and how he was already planning trips and events we would experience together. I was excited. Aunt Mollie was excited. This was going to be GREAT!

We headed home early Sunday morning. Jim dropped me off in Colorado City then drove with Sam on to Lubbock to pick up the three C's that evening. Again, it was Jim's turn to have the boys. I was amazed how quickly the turnovers seemed to occur. Was one week going to be enough time for me to regroup from having the triplets? Well, I had no choice in that matter. I was going to have to manage…somehow.

Things were coming down to the wire. The Christmas programs were scheduled for the coming weekend, and then the movers would be coming the next week to move me to Lubbock. Instead of me driving to Lubbock, Jim planned to bring the boys to Colorado City so they could attend the recital and church service. I felt really nervous about that, especially since they had not fully learned the meaning of "bottoms glued to the pews." However, I agreed for them to come, because with Sam in the picture, he could help some with the boys while Jim helped me with the final preparations.

Both Christmas productions were very successful. I can remember the organist saying, "Wow, Lynette. You really went out with a bang!" I had already let the pastor know that this would be my last Sunday as music director. I also ended my relationships with my piano students. My last week in Colorado City was a sad but happy time—a time to reflect over the last eight years, but also a time to be joyful over the thought of a bright happy future with my new family.

What happened next should be deemed as entirely impossible for a member of the human race to accomplish. On Wednesday morning, the movers arrived to move all my belongings to Lubbock. Since we had two households of furniture, we had to store some of mine and some of Jim's in a storage unit, then take what was left over and try to nestle it into one house.

During the move, I lost my voice. Just when I needed to be barking orders and giving instructions, I couldn't talk. Jim and I had gone room by room and made a list of what was to stay and what was to go, but the movers couldn't decipher that, and Jim couldn't really remember. By the time we finished and had everything put in storage, it was nearly 11:00 p.m. We didn't get to bed until after midnight that night.

Sam had two more half days of school before the holidays, and without thinking, I had offered to keep the boys for those two afternoons after school. Thursday morning came way too early. Jim offered to take Sam to school so I could start organizing. The movers had just dumped the "extra little stuff" in the garage and it was my job to get that cleaned out and taken to the storeroom in Jim's back yard. I was on a mission. I wanted to be able to get at least one car in the garage in case we had bad weather. Also, my family was to arrive on Friday afternoon for the rehearsal dinner, minus the rehearsal. Remember, we were both old pros at marriage ceremonies, so we obviously did not need any practice. Just for reference, do not ever think that way. Wedding rehearsals are almost always a requirement. One never knows what could happen.

But wait! I still couldn't talk nor did I feel good. So between cleaning out the garage, taking care of the boys, and planning dinner for Saturday night, I had to find an unknown doctor in a strange place that would perform a miracle and get my voice back before the next morning. After all, how could I get married if I couldn't say, "I do"?

I found an independent emergency clinic. The doctor on staff gave me a high-powered shot of antibiotic, told me to drink plenty of fluids, go home, and get some rest. Yeah, right. Getting rest before Saturday seemed impossible. The wedding was set for 3:00 in the afternoon, and I knew there would be no peace until that night, when it was over and Jim and I were alone.

Aunt Mollie and Uncle Dee weren't planning to arrive at Jim's until around noon on Friday. Aunt Mollie was a smart, savvy woman. She knew if she got there any earlier, I would put her to work. She was right because the minute she arrived, I immediately put her to work re-covering a window seat that I thought had to be done before that evening. Aunt Mollie had given me her older Singer sewing machine, and I knew she could operate it. I had already bought the material, so she got to work. My voice was not quite back yet, but she managed to comprehend my instructions. She completed the window seat in about three hours, and it was beautiful. No sweat! It was about 2:00 p.m., and dinner wasn't until 7:00. I was thinking clearly.

Believe it or not, everything was done, and the house even decorated for Christmas. One of the weeks while I had been gone, Sam and Jim had put up lights on the outside of the house, and Thanksgiving weekend, Jim and the boys had put up the tree.

The evening of the rehearsal dinner, we served an easy meal of lasagna, salad, and French bread. And since there were twenty-two of us, we unanimously decided on paper plates. Large pitchers of ice tea were ready, and Jim stopped at the store on his way home from work and picked up extra ice.

We all shared an extra special evening. I was able to meet Jim's two older sons, Josh and Jon, and my entire family got to meet Jim's family. I was exhausted but beaming. When the evening wound down and people left to go to the hotel, I followed with my packed bags. I was not going to let Jim see me the day of the wedding until I walked down the aisle. Sam came to the hotel with me. For the last night of bachelorhood, Jim had the triplets by himself for bedtime and prayers.

I got to bed about midnight that night and slept like a log. Since everything had been done on my part, I could sleep late. Aunt Mollie was in charge of the reception, but she was super organized. Derek, my oldest son, handled picking up the cake at the grocery store. I was planning on being at the church about 1:00 p.m. I was not needed but figured it would keep my sanity in check.

It looked like this new adventure in my life was really going to happen. Soon, Jim and I would be married. I would be a newlywed living in Lubbock, Texas and the proud stepmother of triplets, plus Josh and Jon.

Everything seemed perfect. You see, I was still thinking...

Six

Even though I had a chance to sleep late on my wedding day, it didn't happen. How could it? This was the most exciting day of my life, and it was going to be something I would remember for many years to come. For the most part, things seemed pretty normal. However, there were some special happenings that deserve mentioning. Did you know that the wind has a tendency to blow in West Texas? Ordinarily, it blows almost every day in the spring, but sometimes gusts can kick up at the most inopportune times. When I got to the church that Saturday afternoon, the wind was fierce, blowing 40-50MPH and stirring dust in the air. I went to get my bag and as I popped the trunk, the lid almost flew off the hinges. Carrying our necessities for the day, Sam and I struggled through the tempest to reach the front door. But, for a reason only known to God, the wind finally stopped minutes before guests started arriving. I thanked God for His grace and blessings.

Back when I was living in Colorado City, word had spread fast through the small town that I was a bit musical, so my pastor offered me the job of music director at the church. I jumped on that! I needed the extra money and knew I could wave my arms to the beat of the music. The job paid $400 a month, and at that point, I welcomed the extra money.

I was given my very own set of keys to the church. While

exploring inside, I found a 3-octave set of hand bells in a closet. As a young child, I had learned to play hand bells, and thoroughly enjoyed the beautiful sounds they made and the fellowship that came along with rehearsals. I had rung bells most of my life. It was my passion. I got permission from our pastor to start a bell choir. I was in my happy place. Well, not quite yet. Trying to recruit members from a small congregation turned out to be torture. There weren't many talented musicians in the small church in Colorado City, but after about a year of struggling, the close friends who played could hold their own. I assured the prospects that all they needed to do was count to four and know their colors. Honestly! With a very persuasive flair, I eventually recruited eleven members, and we became like a very close family. We practiced on Thursday evenings and were known as "TNT," Thursday Night Therapy. We had even begun playing for senior citizens, nursing homes, and special events in the community. It was great! We always laughed, felt good about ourselves and others, and had a wonderful time when we were together.

Weeks before I announced my engagement to Jim during bell choir rehearsal, we had all laughed and joked about toting the choir to Lubbock to play at the wedding. The more I thought about it, the more appealing the idea became. The Methodist church in Lubbock had a bell choir. I asked permission to use their bells, and the idea came to fruition. My small hand-bell choir from First United Methodist Church in Colorado City would be performing in my wedding. How special!

Since the resource of musicians was scarce in Colorado City, I had solicited the wife of the Presbyterian preacher to be a member of our bell choir. We were all bouncing ideas off of each other when one of the bell ringers said, "Wait! There is a Presbyterian amongst us!" No, that could not happen. Presbyterians were not a part of the Methodist family. We would have to disguise her as a Methodist by having her arrive with a covered dish in hand. We all laughed, but they knew I was serious. It wasn't long before everyone was on board and agreed. I could not believe they were coming, but that afternoon they all showed up in the church van, ready to ring. Dennie Treat, the marriage coordinator, had set up the bells, table, and covers, and we were in business.

The bell choir was a bit shocked when I told them we would play "Carol of the Bells" to ring at our wedding as a tribute to God and our marriage. With a little persuasion and many compliments, I convinced them it was the thing to do. They had played "Carol of the Bells" for the Christmas program at church, did well and were confident they could do it again. To introduce something new would never have done. I was lucky that we had decided to wed before Christmas, as the church was decorated and filled with poinsettias, and the bells would be perfect.

As the bell choir and other out-of-town guests began arriving at the church, I had a hard time staying in my dressing room. I wanted to see everyone and visit. This was a bad choice, because even though I had told Jim not to arrive until 2:30 p.m., he and the triplets came early. There I was standing right in the middle of the hall when he walked in the door. Didn't he know it was bad luck to see the bride before the wedding? I dashed away, but not before he saw me. I was NOT going to be superstitious. Surely this had happened to other brides and they survived. We would just have to pretend he never saw me.

The moments ticked away and it was almost time for me to walk down the aisle. I wanted all the boys to be involved in the wedding, and with four boys, we had to be creative. Sam had the hardest job of all. He was the first one to walk down the aisle. He was the only acolyte and the florist had failed to make sure all the wicks were flame ready. It took him forever to light all those candles. The organist kept playing, and I'm sure Sam's arms were just about ready to drop off. This particular event should have only lasted a few minutes, but it seemed an eternity. I could almost feel a sigh of relief from the guests as he finally lit the last candle.

We've all heard of flower girls, but we had young potpourri peddlers at our wedding. Cody and Caleb were the peddlers, spreading Christmas potpourri instead of petals as they made their way down the aisle. Cooper performed the duty of ring bearer. And just to make sure he didn't drop the ring, I had secured it with a single thread and included a ribbon just for show. I made sure that Jim knew he would have to break the thread to get the ring off the pillow. I was almost certain that a small boy would not be able to keep from playing with a gold ribbon, so it made sense to just give it a little extra security. That was probably a wrong decision.

Finally, it was my turn to walk down the aisle. Once again, Jim's eyes sparkled as our eyes met and he watched me enter the sanctuary on Derek's arm. My oldest son has always been a slowpoke, but for some reason, he was literally racing us down the aisle. I asked him to slow down. In past times when we had gone shopping, he always told me to slow down, asking if I was in a hurry. Today, I wanted this moment to last as long as possible. Wedding ceremonies are always so fast if you aren't Catholic. We had put a lot of work into our wedding and I didn't want it to just zip by.

Derek and I made it to the front as the organist finished playing Pachelbel's wedding song. Jon and Josh stood on Jim's side, and Derek and Sam stood on my side. The C's were supposed to be standing with Jon and Josh, but instead they were everywhere else. Cody lay down on the floor, sliding around on his back, and I spotted Cooper walking on the padded altar, carrying the ring pillow down by his side. Caleb was trying to corral his brothers. He attempted to rein Cooper back to where he was supposed to be standing and tried to peel Cody off the floor. I struggled to pay attention to what Monte, my heroic preacher, was saying. I could feel my face turning red and wanted it all to end. I could not take in what the ceremony entailed; it was all I could do to stand still and wait to hear the words, "I now pronounce you man and wife."

Sometime after our vows, it was time for the bells to ring. I left my place next to Jim at the front of the sanctuary and made my way to the side altar area where the bells were set up. The bell members made their way to the tables.

*Ring, ring, ring-a-ling-ling...*they were doing great! I was proud of my little bell choir from Colorado City. And then...it began to fall apart. Someone missed a bell and threw the others off. No one was on time, and everyone seemed lost. Somehow, someway, we all finished together and the ending made a beautiful, unified chord. At that moment, I knew God was present and blessing our marriage.

As I made my way back to Jim at the front, I noticed that all the boys were standing in place. After a few more words from the pastor, Jim yanked the rings off of the pillow Cooper held. And finally the man I said would never marry, whom I had fallen utterly in love with, put the ring on my finger. I put a ring on his, then Monte said those words I had longed to hear: "I now pronounce you man and wife." Jim and I kissed. The guests applauded. I was officially Mrs. Jim Albright, and the stepmother of five new sons. Wow.

After the ceremony, we posed for pictures. It took a while to get a good one of all the family, but we finally managed. The wedding photos turned out pretty good in spite of the fact that Cooper couldn't stand still and Cody looked like he was about to fall over. Jim and I didn't care. We were married and that was all that mattered.

The reception was wonderful. Aunt Mollie had arranged everything, and my sisters, Caye and Carole, served the food. We didn't have a big dinner and dance, because we had several out-of-town guests and we wanted them to be able to travel home, if they preferred. I got to meet some of Jim's close friends and colleagues from the law community and from school. There were also some members of the church I had met while visiting our church, and it was nice to know we had their support.

While accepting congratulations and answering questions from some of these people, from the corner of my eye I saw Aunt Mollie chasing Cooper. She had set throw-away-cameras on each of the tables, and Jim had created a unique little poem that said, "Special memories are being made today. If you see one, pick me up and snap away." Well, Cooper thought that meant him! He was taking pictures of the floor, people's feet, the ceiling, anything that moved, and anything that didn't move. No sooner than Aunt Mollie would take one camera from him and set it back on the table, he would run to a nearby table and pick up another one. We got a few good pictures out of them, but I am not sure providing cameras was worth the exasperation that Aunt Mollie experienced that day.

As a new stepmom, I could see I had a job ahead of me, even if I was only going to have the triplets every other week. They didn't know exactly what discipline was, and they had no respect for authority or elders. It was going to be a battle zone for a while until they learned what I expected, what they could do and couldn't do, and who was boss. Apparently, Jim had only been a caretaker and had never practiced being a disciplinarian. I knew the change was imperative if they were going to survive throughout their school years and through the rest of their lives as adults.

Between meeting people, I spotted my bell choir off to the

side of the garden room. I couldn't wait to talk to them. I almost ran with open arms. To me, it was so special for them to make the trip and play bells during the ceremony. They gave me lots of hugs, congratulations, and more hugs. I loved every one of them. They were all apologizing for their mistakes during their performance, but to me, their bell ringing was beautiful music from my dear friends. I couldn't have been happier than I was at that moment. I was going to miss every one of them very, very much.

When the time came to cut the cake, Jim and I picked up the knife and proceeded to cut our piece, but that nut wouldn't crack. That cake was hard as a rock. He thought I was pulling back as he was pushing down. I thought Jim was the culprit. At the beginning of our relationship, I had told him that 99.9% of the things that go wrong would be his fault. Surely, this was one of them.

Firmly, I said, "Stop it."

He said, "Stop what?"

"Push down!"

"I am!"

What's the deal? I wondered.

Then, it occurred to me: the cake was frozen! I laughed and tried to explain to him that the grocery store baker had stored it frozen to keep the icing from sliding off, but apparently we had not given the cake enough time to thaw. No one had unboxed it until the reception. I had trouble getting Jim to understand but we finally axed a piece out and fed each other bits of ice-cake in the traditional way. We handed the fancy wedding knife to my sister, Caye, to serve the other guests. Aunt Mollie had seen what was happening and she was on it. She arrived within seconds with a butcher knife.

The reception wound down, and it was time for us to leave. All of my family had traveled here, so I reserved a block of rooms with a local hotel. Caye and her husband, Russ, were taking Sam and their daughter, Christine, to the hotel to stay for the night. Jim's son, Jon, had agreed to take the triplets to their mother's. She had kindly agreed to keep them on our wedding night, but the plans were to pick them up the next morning in time to go to church. My goodness, my life had changed in a hurry. I wasn't even going to get to spend twenty-four hours alone with my new husband.

Jim and I said our goodbyes to relatives and friends, and

headed out the door. Through all the chaos that day, we made some sweet memories. As Jim and I traveled to our hotel, we talked about the happenings and discounted the less-than-perfect events. Many weddings had survived much worse, and the fact of the matter was that we were finally married. No more long road trips and no more being apart. We were united as one under God, and that was very comforting.

* * *

At the hotel, Jim and I changed clothes and headed down to the atrium to visit with my family. None of Jim's family had come to the wedding except for Jon, Josh, and the triplets, and none of them were staying overnight at the hotel. Later, I realized that it was very special that Jon and Josh had attended.

We had all agreed to meet in the lobby for happy hour before Jim and I went to dinner for our wedding night, and it was great. Even my mom had come, despite her struggle with Alzheimer's. We all talked about the events of the day and laughed about the triplets' ordeal with the cameras, the frozen cake, and even the fact that Cody was mopping the floor with his back during the ceremony. We visited for about an hour, and then Jim and I went to dinner. He had picked a very romantic place for our first evening together as husband and wife. I loved this man so very much!

The Italian restaurant was owned by two brothers from New York City. Jim was a regular there, and they treated us like royalty. They brought us a bottle of their best champagne in a bucket of ice to toast our wedding. The gesture was very special, but being a recovered alcoholic, I didn't dare take a sip. I pretended and let Jim drink the whole bottle. We had a wonderful time, and he had a slight buzz by the end of the meal, so I drove us back to the hotel. One nice thing about not ever drinking…there's always a designated driver in the family, and it is yours truly.

Jim was extremely tired, and I felt a little weary myself. The last few weeks had been just a tad stressful, and exhaustion set in. We were both elated to be married and to have all the chaos of the last few weeks behind us.

Seven

We slept soundly that night and almost overslept the next morning. We were supposed to be checked out and on our way to pick up the boys for church by 9:00. Why did I always put myself in a position to be stressed? Would I ever learn?

Since Sam stayed in my sister's hotel room, we gathered him up and said our goodbyes to my family. Tears welled up in my eyes and my stomach knotted as I hugged my mom, Aunt Mollie, Uncle Dee, Caye, Carole, and Scott, my little brother.

The triplets were ready when we arrived at their mother's house and they all piled into the van. Seatbelts clicked and the four boys chatted excitedly that they were all now brothers. I relished their smiles and laughter. We were now a family indeed. I wondered how long this happiness would last and when all the bickering would begin. What was going to happen when all the newness wore off and Sam became just a bossy intruder? Only time would tell...

Before going into the church, I reminded them how we expected them to behave: bottoms on the pew, glued to the seat. No sitting in Dad's lap. No climbing over pews. No crawling under pews. No walking out in the aisle. They were to stand when we stood and sit when we sat. While the church provided children's kits filled with busy work, a six-year-old's attention span isn't very long. I could also see that sometimes

Sam was a fuel injector when it came to stirring things up at inappropriate times.

We arrived at church and took all the children to their prospective Sunday school classes. Jim and I headed to the class we had attended several times before, but I wanted to eventually start visiting other classes and find one where we felt comfortable and fit in. Horror struck me as we walked in the door and Dave Treat was perched ready to teach.

We had failed to invite him and Dennie to the wedding!

Several times over the last few months, as we were putting together the guest list, I had asked Jim if he had included the Treats. He kept saying, "I think so," and I kept saying, "Make sure." Sure enough, they got left off of the list. I wanted to crawl through the cracks in the floor. I know my face was red and I could not muster up the guts to say anything to Dave.

On the way to the sanctuary, we ran into Dennie in the hall, and of course, since she was the wedding consultant, she wanted to know how it went. Again, I wanted to crawl in a hole. I said it was very nice and thanked her for all the help, and then I tried to explain. Have you ever noticed how hard it is to explain to someone why they weren't invited to a special occasion? I felt like my mouth was full of feet.

She kept saying, "It's okay," but I wasn't okay with it. Right then and there, I told myself we were going to have to invite them to dinner as soon as we could. I was on a mission to make things right.

The Three C's behavior during the service was a little better, but not much. I could see that I was going to have to figure out consequences when the boys didn't follow instructions. At least they weren't climbing over and under pews, but Cooper was still walking out in the aisle. No one wanted me to sit by Jim. Whoever wasn't sitting next to Jim wanted to be sitting on his lap. It seemed as though we played musical chairs throughout the service, and once again, after all was said and done, I was exhausted. Things were going to have to change!

* * *

The boys stayed at our house that Sunday afternoon and would be going back to their mom's at 6:00 that evening. This was her year to have the Three C's for Christmas, but they would come to our house for a visit on Christmas Day to open presents from us and Santa Claus.

Jim and their mother had a system, and it seemed to work pretty well. For Christmas, the parents bought gifts for everyone and everything belonged to everyone. There were no names on any of the gifts; whatever gift Cody opened was also Cooper's and Caleb's. The triplets shared the toys and games equally. Pretty good, huh? Their mother had gone to a close-out warehouse and bought tons of toys. Of course, Sam had always gotten his own presents, so the combination of our gift-giving traditions was going to be very interesting. I wondered if the triplets were going to think what was Sam's was theirs, too.

Over the next several days, Jim and I went shopping for Jon, Josh, and Derek. They were all going to be in town for the holidays, and I had invited them for Christmas dinner. I was still exhausted from the wedding, but I could see the light at the end of the tunnel. I knew if I could just get through Christmas, I would be okay. Jim and I were going on our honeymoon the next week where I could get away from it all, eat out all the time, and sleep until noon. I couldn't wait.

Surprisingly enough, Christmas Day turned out okay. The toy thing went pretty smoothly, and the triplets didn't seem too interested in Sam's gifts. Sam was more interested in their gifts, and since it didn't seem like a big issue to share, the Three

C's treated him like one of the family. The older boys appeared to enjoy their gifts, too, and I would say our first blended-family Christmas was a success. Derek, Jon, and Josh even took time to check out the games and toys, and actually interacted with their brothers.

I cried a little as Derek gave me a big hug as he was leaving and said, "I love you, Mom." The newly expanded Albright family was off to a great start.

PART TWO

Adventures in Stepmothering

Eight

The next few days were busy getting ready for our trip. Jim belonged to an association through his job with Tech. Every year, they had a conference in a different city after Christmas, before classes started for the second semester. This year, they had chosen Las Vegas for the location, and Jim and I decided to just treat it as our honeymoon. He would have to be in sessions part of the days, but we would have evenings free to do as we pleased. While he was busy, I would use my free time to write thank-you notes and read.

Our church scheduled a young lady, Sara, to stay with Sam through the weekend, and then she would be in charge of the triplets, too, starting on Monday, since we wouldn't be back until Wednesday. Sam was a little nervous about the situation, but Jim and I trusted all would be fine. I was sure after Sam got used to Sara, he would be fine, too. All these adjustments were mind-boggling. I just had to have faith in God that He would provide. God's faithfulness is real. I just had to remember.

Ah, the honeymoon. Jim was the perfect gentleman and so attentive. He loaded and unloaded my luggage, opened doors for me, and always had his hand on the small of my back whenever we walked together. You know...all of those little things that are so amazing after you have been single for quite some time, and not expecting such attentive gestures.

When we arrived in Las Vegas, all of the arrangements had been made. Our room was exquisite, complete with a hot tub for two. This lady from small-town Colorado City had not had much experience with Jacuzzis! I knew I would have to check this out later.

For the first night in Las Vegas, Jim made reservations at the best restaurant located within the hotel where we were staying. He knew my favorite food was ribeye steak, and this was definitely a first-rate steakhouse. He had pre-arranged for a quiet table for two in a secluded corner, and there was an vase of yellow roses (my favorite) on the table when we arrived. It seemed like the entire waitstaff were there for us. After a fabulous dinner, the restaurant allowed us to take the bouquet of roses with us, which landed a home on the side table in our room. Once again, Jim had planned every little detail, and I felt taken care of.

The next day was mine to spend as I pleased. Jim had training sessions every day, because this was a "working" holiday. However, before he left, he ordered room service for me, and I indulged in lounging until about 1:00 p.m. Then, I was off to explore Las Vegas and go shopping. I wanted to buy almost everything I saw, but I settled on two scented candles for our experience in the hot tub. Yes, it seemed I was close to Heaven.

That evening, Jim arrived and ordered a couple of cocktails for himself. We exchanged stories about the day, and then made arrangements for the evening activities. As a wedding present, my youngest brother, Scott, had bought us tickets to the Cirque du Soleil show, "O." After dinner at another fabulous restaurant, we made our way to the theatre. It was absolutely amazing! The performances were astonishing and nothing like I had ever seen before. People were doing all kinds of contortions (unlike a human being), doing high dives into a pool that seemed to be inches in depth, and unbelievable acrobatic tricks. What an experience!

It was late when we returned to our room, but I was determined to try out that hot tub. As I filled the tub, I lit the scented candles, and set them at the side of the tub. I am not going into a lot of detail here; you can fill in the blanks. However, I will say it was a very special night for me, and one I will remember forever.

One more day and evening in Las Vegas, and then it would be time to go home. I walked the strip and saw things I had never seen before: street performers, dancing girls providing a photograph with anyone willing to pay a fee, and those human statues. People painted from head to in gold or silver were able to stay motionless for hours. I can't stay still for 10 minutes!

That afternoon, I found the pool and thoroughly enjoyed people watching. I saw more skin that day…some of which I did not want to see. No one was in the pool; it was much too cool. However, I soaked up some sun and much needed vitamin D. A little sun has always made me feel more attractive, and I was really looking forward to being with Jim that evening.

Since I was a small-town girl, I had never gambled in all my life. Jim was a pro at black jack, and he was convinced he would teach me and try my luck at the tables. He had brought a deck of cards (so thoughtful!) so when he got in from his training classes and after he ordered a few cocktails, I had a lesson in the room before venturing out for dinner and gambling. Seemed simple enough…this was going to be fun.

We jumped in a cab from the hotel, and while heading downtown, Jim explained that the Black Jack dealers were friendlier, and loved to have newbies at their tables. Really? This I would have to see.

The cab dropped us off at Freemont Street, and I became starstruck. They call it "the Freemont Street Experience." We got there just in time to see the amazing light show that appears above the street on a canopy. The scene is all computerized, and if you haven't seen it, you must!

After the show, we walked to Binion's for dinner. Jim had made a reservation for us and again, we had a very romantic table for two with a view of the city. The steak was amazing and the service was excellent. During dinner, Jim laid his hand on mine and said, "I love you so very much. We are going to have a great life together." Once again, his eyes said it all.

Time to gamble! We made our way downstairs and found the Black Jack tables. Jim spotted an empty table, and we sat down and met the dealer. I lost all my gambling money in an hour, but Jim managed to win $500. Even though the dealer was full of charm and so very nice, this was just not my game. Jim and I laughed, arm in arm, as we walked to the room. How could I have been so unlucky at Black Jack?

Every evening we were in Las Vegas, Jim would arrive at the room with a gift. One evening, a gold bracelet, the next, perfume. Jim was so romantic. I truly felt my prince had arrived. Every moment of our honeymoon seemed magical, and I didn't want that to end.

Back home, Sara did a wonderful job watching over Sam and the triplets, and Jim and I got the rest we needed. We were happy newlyweds, and a couple whose future looked so bright. My only complaint was that the trip ended too quickly. I wish we could have stayed a few more days, but the responsibilities back home were calling our names. As people say, "Back to real." I felt reality set in as we boarded the plane. My duties as mother and stepmother were about to resume. During the flight home, I couldn't help but dread having four little boys under foot.

When we arrived in Lubbock, we called Sara to let her know we were on our way. She had the boys make "Welcome home!" signs, and they all greeted us with hand-drawn cards and pictures. Such a delightful homecoming! All of the boys were happy and smiling. Right then, I just knew our new life together was going to wonderful. And I could see in Sam's eyes that he knew it too.

* * *

The week of our honeymoon, the Three C's and Sam were under our supervision until school started the next week. We could have put them in daycare, but I didn't want to send Sam, and it didn't seem fair to keep the boys apart, since they wanted to be together. We would manage somehow, and as long as I knew they would be back at their mother's the following week and Sam would be back in school, we would get through our first week together as a blended family.

Jim still had a few days off from work, so at least I had his help. The trouble with me was *letting* him help. I have always known that my way of doing anything was the best, and I had a terrible tendency to take control. Jim had been doing "Daddy day care" for three years every other week, but he just wasn't doing it right! The triplets were going to have to learn to do things for themselves: dress themselves, bath themselves, and brush their own teeth. And they were going to learn how to eat vegetables with a fork and mashed potatoes with a spoon. As I headed to the grocery store to get milk and supplies, I tried to come up with some ideas. This was not going to be easy.

Mashed potatoes were going to be a staple, since they ate French fries and tater tots. But wait. Tater tots and French fries were potatoes, right? Check. I added them to my grocery list. They may taste a little different than fast food, but didn't they look the same? Carrots! Didn't every little kid like carrots? I thought Bugs Bunny was a role model. Surely, they would like carrots. Apples and bananas were a must. Celery always went well with peanut butter, but cucumbers and broccoli were almost certain to be failures. Sam had eaten all these things as snacks, and my only salvation was his influence on the triplets' taste buds. With any luck, they would see Sam's ways and follow suit. I hoped for a miracle.

I decided to have meatloaf, tater tots, and glazed carrots for dinner. My mom had given me a bread-making machine a few years ago, and I intended to start using it regularly. Surely the Three C's liked bread because they ate hot dogs and hamburgers all the time. Wait, that's not entirely true. Cody only liked hot dogs and Caleb and Cooper only liked hamburgers, but only meat and bread. Would I ever get this all straight? Hopefully, that wouldn't be necessary because soon everyone would be eating the same thing at every meal, and it wasn't going to be just hot dogs or hamburgers.

When I returned home that afternoon, Jim and all four boys came to unload and help put up groceries. The questions from the boys were overwhelming.

"What's this?"

"Do we have to eat these?"

"What do you do with this?"

"Do humans even eat these?"

"Yes, Yes," I said. "Now go play. You will see at dinner."

Dinner Time! The triplets said the tater tots were strange because they didn't come out of a box or a paper sack. Getting them to understand the concept of meatloaf proved to be challenging.

Then Cooper acknowledged that meatloaf was actually a hamburger patty presented a different way, so he was my hero that evening. The glazed carrots had to be *forced*, and I literally mean forced. I even tried calling them "candied carrots." No dice. Sam was the only one to put glazed carrots in his mouth.

The Three C's did not know what these orange vegetables were, and they said the bread was weird. It didn't look like a hot dog bun nor a hamburger bun. We also had another lesson on the use of utensils, and it didn't go very well. Cutting meatloaf themselves was too much to ask, and not one triplet was interested in trying to use a spoon. They found it easier to pick up the meatloaf by hand and eat it like pizza. I wasn't surprised, but I remained determined. We had another brutal lesson on forks and knives, and I knew this was going to take a very long time and a great deal of patience.

I had prepared a dessert as a form of bribery. Even though I told the boys they couldn't have dessert until they at least tried everything on their plate, my bribe didn't work. No way was Cody going to put a carrot in his mouth, and the tater tots didn't taste right to Cooper. Very calmly, I got up and walked around the table between Caleb and Sam. I put a carrot on Caleb's fork, placed his fingers around the fork in the correct manner, and told him to put it in his mouth. I told Sam to do the same thing, as he said, "Come on guys. This stuff is good! Just try." Sam was getting a little nervous at this point.

I said to Caleb again, "Put it in your mouth, now."

He had a somewhat fearful look on his face as he watched Sam put his carrot in his mouth. Jim watched silently and some of the boys squirmed.

"Now, Caleb." I said it again louder, "NOW, Caleb!" Finally, I took his hand and forced the forked carrot to his mouth. His lips stayed closed, jaw locked. "Open your mouth, Caleb." Half-opened, I shoved the carrot in and released his hand.

His face turned stone-cold sober, but still, he did not move or chew.

I looked at Cooper. "Try a carrot, Cooper."

He stared at me.

"Try a tater tot, Caleb."

He blinked. How could he move on to a tater tot? He had not even chewed the carrot yet! This was maddening.

I had to force a carrot into Cody's mouth, too. When Cooper saw me rounding the table to assist him next, he quickly picked up a piece of meatloaf and put it in his mouth. I guess he figured if he was eating something, he was safe from the wicked stepmother.

As the moments passed during our battle of wills, Cody's mouth still had not moved. He was determined not to chew, much less swallow that carrot. Caleb continued to hold his carrot in his mouth, and Cooper had not picked up a utensil. This was a dead heat. Who was going to win?

Instead of bringing this to a full-blown, all-out war, I let it go. Everyone ate the meatloaf, and Cooper ate the bread, but all Three C's left the vegetables untouched, except for the forced carrot. Cody excused himself to go to the bathroom, so I knew that carrot was going down the toilet. Sam didn't eat all of his servings, but he at least ate a little of everything.

I got up to clear the table and Jim rose to help me. It was my intention to make the triplets sit at the table and watch us eat vanilla ice cream with chocolate syrup, but I couldn't do it. I didn't want to alienate them completely in just the first week, so we let them go play while we enjoyed our ice cream. Besides, I just had to deal with this through the end of this week, and then they would be back with their mother.

Jim was helping me clean up the kitchen and, once again, I couldn't help but notice how much food was going down the disposal. Before the meal, I had decided to try to keep things simple. I was smart enough not to flirt with disaster, so Jim and I filled the plates. As usual, he had given them too many carrots and an overabundance of mashed potatoes. It was also a known fact that milk was to be served with every meal, and now I was dumping glass after glass down the sink.

Once again, I gently asked Jim if he thought it would be a good idea if, from now on, we only filled the glasses half full. I said, "Then maybe most of the milk we buy each week wouldn't end up down the drain."

We laughed and found humor in the evening and what had happened during the meal, because you see, we were still newlyweds and the honeymoon was not over! I was trying to think clearly and could see some hardships ahead, but could also clearly see a positive future.

As we started on the next task of tidying up and getting the boys bathed and ready for bed, I asked Jim if he thought Cody had ever swallowed that carrot. We both paused a moment and wondered. I told Jim what I suspected, but he said, "Cody would never think of doing that."

Oh, yeah? Let's bet on it. I let it go and didn't say anything more, but I was already working on a solution.

From time to time, all children need guidance, some more than others. These boys were no exception, and I was willing to put in the extra effort to make this blended family work. Why? Because I wanted the man!

Nine

About two months before we were married, Jim broke a tendon in the middle finger of his left hand playing basketball with the professors during his lunch hour. When he called and explained what had happened, it did not seem like that big of a deal, but later seeing the damaged finger made my heart skip a beat. If it was not braced 24/7, the finger just flopped and hung almost like there was no tendon. It was as if the end joint was not attached at all.

I insisted he see a hand specialist, and she explained the only way the finger would get better was if the tendon reattached itself. This meant the finger had to stay in a papoose-type cast that kept it totally straight for at least three months. Can you even imagine how hard it would be to keep it clean, dry, and properly bandaged while taking care of three young boys?

Jim tried to hide that finger in all of our wedding pictures, and as a result, it looked like he had no middle finger at all. Poor guy!

One evening Jim called and was totally exasperated. He was tired of getting it wet and tired of trying to bandage it himself. I suggested gloves, but finding gloves that would fit over that enlarged middle finger was impossible. At times, especially when showering, he would use a rubber band and a plastic bag over his left hand, which was doable, but very awkward.

That first night living with him, I asked what he was doing to get his hand wet all the time.

He said, "Bathing the boys."

What? He was bathing the boys. Okay.

"You mean they cannot bathe themselves?"

"Well, no."

At this point, I wanted to tell him it was because he had never taught them, but I was too nice. "Jim. They are six years old. They can bathe themselves."

"No, they can't."

"YES, they can." I told him to pretend he was a coach, a hand's off coach, and to just tell them step by step what to do. Even though it was easier to do it himself, eventually they were going to have to learn how to bathe themselves. I suggested he do it right then, because I knew he would not be allowed to stay with them in the freshman dorm when they started college. I didn't really know what had been going on at bath time since that conversation, so after dinner when Jim said, "Okay, boys, time for your bath," I waited and watched. While he went to fill the tub, the Three C's ran to the utility room and totally stripped. After leaving their clothes on the floor in front of the washer, they ran naked to the bathroom and all crawled into the tub.

A few weeks before, during the move to Lubbock, Jim had caught that finger in my ice chest and ripped off the bandage and papoose in one swift movement. We both were stunned and looked at the finger, but realized at that point, it was probably as good as it was ever going to get. The tendon appeared to be halfway attached, so it didn't totally flop anymore. It just sort of hung there…bent. We were both very tired of babysitting that finger, changing bandages, and returning week after week to the hand specialist, hoping it would get better. By the time I observed the bathing ritual that evening, the bandage was a thing of the past.

Even as I watched, Jim still bathed them one by one. On his knees, he shampooed their hair, sponged down body parts, used a plastic pitcher to rinse them off, while the triplets played with bath toys and complained constantly of getting water in their eyes. He picked up Cooper first, toweled him dry, and dressed him in his underwear and pajamas. Jim went to Caleb next and performed the same ritual, one by one, until they were all clean, dry, and dressed. Cody was last, and before Jim let him go play with the other boys, he got a toothbrush out, put a gob of toothpaste on it, and proceeded to brush Cody's teeth. Cody wailed the whole time. There was no misunderstanding that he didn't like to have his teeth brushed. No wonder the other boys disappeared after bath time. You would have thought Cody was being tortured. After that ordeal, Jim set out to find one of the other boys. I'm sure they were hiding.

I asked Cody if getting his teeth brushed was really that bad, and all he could do was nod, with big alligator tears in his eyes. I gave him a one-sided hug and let him wander off. Jim soon reappeared with Cooper, his next victim. From his tortured cries, you would have thought that Cooper's left arm was being cut off. Caleb just wanted his dad's love and approval, but I could still tell brushing teeth was not his favorite activity. One by one they were all done. Again, Jim performed the whole ritual. What should have taken minutes took half an hour. It was almost more than I could bear to keep my mouth shut. After all, change takes time and they would soon be back at their mother's. All I had to do was last the rest of the week and I was halfway there.

That night was still pretty early and not quite time for bed, so we allowed the boys some more free time while I sent Sam to the shower to get ready for bed.

He whined, "Mom, no!"

"Yes, Sam." I told him if he hurried and didn't lollygag around, he would have time to play with the Three C's before they had to go to bed. He reluctantly headed to the bathroom. Jim stepped out loaded up with towels as Sam stepped in. I closed the door behind him and told Sam to hurry.

Jim headed to the utility room, and I followed. He picked up all of the clothes on the floor, loaded them into the washer with the towels, added some soap, and turned it on. I didn't see what wash setting he used, but I instantly knew why all the white socks were blue. Jim added his dirties to the mix and asked me if I had any. No, thanks! I didn't want blue socks. I also quickly understood why he turned his dress socks inside out. It was to keep the towel fuzzies from collecting on the outside of his good socks. My goodness. As strange as it was, this man certainly had a system.

Sam came out of the shower in no time and we talked the boys into all crawling into our king size bed for reading. No one argued. I wasn't really fond of king beds and had expressed to Jim my wish to change out his for a queen size. For one split second, I thought it would be silly to change, but seeing the whole family piled onto our bed, I began to think clearly. Yes, we would have to downsize to a queen. No way was this going to be an every night ordeal. Jim and I were still newlyweds and

I certainly wanted to maintain that glow as long as possible. I knew I would have to work really hard to keep all these boys from cutting it short.

After about thirty minutes of bedtime stories, it was time to circle up for prayers. The few times I had been there at bedtime, we had all stood in a circle holding hands as we said our prayers. The boys took turns; sometimes more than one said a prayer. Jim always closed with his own prayer. This nightly ritual became a very special time at the end of a busy day. Even during stress, times of conflict, tears, or frustration, our family always ended the day with that quiet time for God. I'm pretty sure those quiet times gave me the courage, wisdom, and strength to face the next day, the next few months, and the next two years.

* * *

Even though some nights were not school nights, Jim and I still needed our quiet time. Since I was living there full time, Jim went back to working more mornings as magistrate for the city. At night, he needed his rest. Sam didn't have to go to bed quite as early as the triplets, but bedtime was still earlier than anyone wanted. To keep whining to a minimum, Sam and I would go to his bedroom to have our quiet time before he went to sleep. Still, I wish I had a dollar for every time I said to the triplets, "Because he's older," trying to justify why Sam got special privileges. I'm sure they got just as tired of hearing that phrase as I was tired of saying it.

With all the boys tucked in for the night, it was bedtime for us at last! But no, there was still that huge load of laundry. Despite feeling weary, I helped Jim turn dress socks right side out, fold towels, and sort blue socks. How did he remember whose jeans were whose, and which shirt belonged to which triplet? We folded and neatly placed them back in the den on the entertainment center used as a dresser. They could hash out whose were whose in the morning. At that point, I was so tired I didn't care.

Day one as a family had been a pretty good day, and the rest of the week went by okay, but I got very frustrated with their eating habits. Either one or two, or all of them, were on medication most of the time, and I figured it had to do with either their eating habits or the fact that they were all using the same tube of toothpaste, and maybe the same toothbrush! I do not know how Jim kept it all straight. I tried to not sweat the small stuff that first week of co-habitation, but after too many days of close proximity, all of the boys began to bicker, and it became apparent that we were going to need a larger house.

I could see the chaos coming. Imagine four boys in one bathroom with one sink trying to brush their teeth at the same time, using the same tube of toothpaste. How many towels do you think they used? They all shared one. No wonder someone was always sick. The evening I had envisioned future chaos, I talked to Jim about buying or building a larger house. To my surprise, he was very receptive. I was so grateful that we were on the same page.

Jim told me his former college roommate, Terry, had been trying to get Jim to build a home for years. Terry was a well-respected home builder in Lubbock. They were still good friends, but Jim had never really considered building a new house until our conversation. Terry would build it for us at cost plus a percentage, and we could use any plan we found suitable for us. How exciting! A new house to start our new lives together was just the ticket. At least I knew it would make me a much happier woman. I was truly doing the happy dance on my way to bed that night.

Ten

Since the boys didn't have school that week and we had more time in the mornings, I presented the prospect of dressing themselves. I will never forget the morning I experimented. Jim had gone back to bed after court, so before he got up and while the Three C's were all glued to Barney, I turned off the television.

"ARGGHHH!" they all whined together.

You would have thought I had blown up the house. I got everyone's attention and told them they were going to dress themselves. I got nothing but blinking, bewildered looks as I explained that they were six years old and other boys their age were dressing themselves. Cody kept his head down as I spoke. Cooper had a blank stare. Caleb was all ears.

No one moved as Sam got up and headed to his bedroom.

Caleb asked, "Where is Sam going?"

I said, "To get dressed."

Caleb thought for a moment and then got up and started toward the open-air dresser. He was willing to try as he picked out his clothes from the stacks, but not without telling me I had misplaced some of the t-shirts.

"Thank-you, Caleb."

Cooper watched as Sam disappeared and then looked at me like I was crazy. Cody, as usual, studied a toy he had in his hands and was not the least bit interested in what I was saying. The odds of this being a successful experience didn't look good. However, I had an idea.

"It's a race! Whoever gets dressed first is the winner and will get a prize!"

I had no idea what that prize was going to be, but I would figure out something. Maybe let one of them sort blue socks or take a bath all by himself. *Don't get too excited*, I told myself.

The Three C's came alive. It was a free-for-all. Arms flailing, eager hands grabbed a pair of jeans or shirt. They almost knocked each other down and cried out as the excitement rose. Watching this sporting competition, I could see who was going to win. Cooper, the biggest, managed to get all his clothes together before Cody, or even Caleb, who had gotten a head start. *Bedlam* is the only word that properly describes the action, and I would have given anything to have caught that moment on video.

Even though the clothes were simple, each boy struggled to get the t-shirts on the right way and fumbled with zipping and buttoning their pants. Poor Cody had the hardest time. They put on their tennis shoes easily because they had Velcro straps, but the socks slowed them down. Cooper was the ultimate winner and Caleb a close second, but poor Cody didn't stand a chance. Everything he did was in slow motion, and even competing in a race couldn't get him up to speed. As soon as he realized he had lost, he found his toy, sunk to the floor, and started to cry.

Goodness! Even though we had some hurt feelings, I realized that these boys could at least dress themselves. Sam came running into the room all dressed, wondering what was up and who had won.

"Cooper!" I said. "Now, what are we going to do about Cody?"

Sam told me how unfair it was for him to have to run to his bedroom to get his clothes, while I was thinking how nice it was for him to have his own private room. Meanwhile, Caleb tried to tell how Cooper had pushed him out of the way to get to the clothes, and Cody sat on the floor and continued to cry. I sat down with Cody and helped him get dressed, as Sam went on about the unfairness for him, and Cooper kept asking me, "So, what's the prize?"

Since I hadn't thought up a prize yet, I didn't answer right away. Besides, I was still helping Cody finish getting dressed.

Growing impatient, Conner yelled, "What's the prize, Mom?"

I had no clue. I know God helped me on this one, so I blurted out without thinking, "How about a popsicle for everyone!"

A look of bewilderment and then joy spread over their little faces except for Sam. He asked, "That's all? That's all we get?"

It was all I could do to keep from strangling him.

Cody rose to his feet slowly and remained quiet as Cooper asked, "But, what do I get for winning?"

I know God helped again as the wisdom came out of my mouth. I diplomatically explained to them that it was their first time, and as far as I was concerned everyone was a winner for getting them dressed.

Cody was quiet for a few seconds until I heard him wailing again, "I WANT MY POPSICLE! ARGGHHH!"

Then Cooper yelled, "But what do *I* get for winning?"

Again, I explained that it was their first time and as far as I was concerned, they were all winners for dressing themselves. Whew! Every day, every event provided a challenge. By the end of the week, I was exhausted and ready for a little quiet time. My battle plan to teach the boys new behaviors was stressful for Jim, too. He tried to take up the slack so I wouldn't be overwhelmed, but it didn't matter. I still felt totally overwhelmed. There was never a dull moment that first week of marriage. If there wasn't joy, laughter, and playful times, there were tears, fights, and arguments. More times than not, I felt like a housekeeper, a nanny, a cook, and a mother. Very few times during that first week did I feel like a loved, cherished, newlywed. Jim treated me wonderfully, but he stayed busy taking care of business, too. With four children under our feet, we rarely had time for ourselves, much less each other. What was I thinking when I decided to marry this man? I had thought I was thinking, but love got in the way.

I didn't think about love when I thought about Cody. What was I going to do about Cody? He was a frustrated, angry little boy, and his personality showed it. He didn't like me or his brothers, and I rarely saw him smile or laugh. Before we had married, I told Jim I was going to need a lot of help with Cody, that it was hard for me to like him. Jim gave me a reassuring hug and told me he understood, but I wondered how I was ever going to like, much less love, Cody. He threw tantrums and mistreated his brothers. He didn't appear to be very bright and showed absolutely no respect for anyone. Jim tried to explain that it probably all stemmed from his low muscle development and how it was slower than his brothers'. Cody didn't crawl for quite some time after his brothers were actively moving about; instead, he pushed himself around on his back with his feet. At the time, Jim didn't think Cody would ever learn to hold his own bottle. Cody didn't start talking until he was about four. Even now, his speech was very hard to understand. His brothers did all the talking for him, and he had dropped behind. Even his motor skills were much to be desired.

I looked at Jim with deep concern. "What are we going to do about Cody?"

* * *

One day before we were married, I had been there to pick up the boys from school. Jim instructed me to wait in the hallway outside the boys' classrooms until they appeared, then lead them out the door and take them to the car. I had never met Cody's teacher before, but she immediately found me and asked if I was picking up the triplets. Before I could introduce myself, she told me Cody was failing. She said half of the first year of school was over, and he still could not read.

"What do you mean he can't read?" I asked. "Full sentences? One syllable words?"

"He just can't read. Period. Not one word."

I was shocked. Did Jim know? Why hadn't he been told? Since I had been a teacher, I was appalled. If Cody was having trouble, something should have been done by now. The problem should have been addressed when he was in kindergarten. I led the boys out of the school in a daze. Cody was not going to fail the first grade. I wouldn't let that happen. I could see the handwriting on the wall. He would be teased mercilessly by other students for being "the dumb one." If he failed first grade, we would have to move him to another school. They couldn't be triplets attending the same school and not be in the same grade.

That evening, I got out some books and sat with Cody at the table. As I opened a book, he turned away, grunted, groaned, pouted, and whined. I literally could not get him to read a single word. The teacher had been right. Cody could not read. My brain was spinning. What were we going to do?

Cody's low muscle development affected his speech. His facial muscles had not fully developed, and even his tongue was incapable of doing the motions needed to speak articulately. Since he couldn't talk clearly and learn and experience phonics, he wasn't going to learn to read. He had been placed in hippotherapy, where the client rides a horse to develop lower muscles and coordination. But as far as I was concerned, he needed speech therapy, *immediately*.

That next week when school started again, I proceeded to the office to speak with the counselor and the assistant principal. I knew there were programs in place within the public schools, but we had to apply to get the help we needed. There would be a lot of testing and paperwork involved, but I was willing to go to any length to see that Cody got the help he needed. I did not want him to be a year or two behind the other boys. At that moment, I made up my mind that I would do everything possible to help Cody catch up with the other boys.

The people at school were a little apprehensive to give out much information, and I could not blame them. Who was this woman claiming to be the triplets' new stepmom? I could tell it would take time to gain their confidence. Fortunately, Cody's teacher had already set the wheels in motion and testing had been scheduled. That day, my goal was to let them know I had Cody's best interest at heart and wanted to do anything I could to expedite the red tape. They told me to get a referral from Cody's doctor and then I could hand-deliver all the necessary paperwork to the administrative offices.

By week two of our marriage, even though the triplets were back at their mom's, I stayed busy. I needed to change my social security information, get a new driver's license made, and pick up Jim for lunch and go to the credit union to get my name put on his account. We had never really talked about finances, but I assumed since I was going to be a stay-at-home mom, he would let me take over the tedious chore of paying bills. Also, I needed to buy groceries and had to have control of a checkbook to feed all these boys.

I began to feel relief knowing that I had left all my single-mom and work duties in Colorado City. As a new wife married to a respected attorney, I envisioned a wonderful life ahead of me. I was having a productive week, recovering beautifully from the previous full week with the triplets, and Sam seemed to be enjoying school. Things were looking good. Jim showed me more attention this week, as we settled into our new life together.

Sunday arrived before I knew it. It was time to get the triplets for church, then rest and soak in all the quiet moments before the Three C's hit the door at 6:00 p.m. However, something really strange hit me that day after church. I began to feel a huge loss and an emptiness I had never experienced, and I am quite sure I was also dreading the return of the triplets. I wasn't ready. *Give me another week!*

What was wrong with me? I was supposed to be happy, but instead I felt very sad. I began to feel like I had totally lost my identity. I didn't have my own home, my own phone, or my own checking account. All I had from my old life was my car. I was no longer a teacher, music director, or piano instructor. My identity had been reduced to only being Sam's mom and Jim's new wife. I'm sure somewhere in there I was getting to be known as the triplets' new stepmom, too, but that was not very comforting.

Like clockwork, the Three C's arrived at 6:00. Luckily, their parents had an agreement to deliver them fed, so I did not have to prepare an evening meal for them. It was a good thing, too, because I wasn't in any shape to try to figure out a menu, nitpick about manners, or force food down throats. On the eve of week three, I couldn't quit crying and poor Jim didn't know what to do. He felt at a loss and wondered why I wasn't as happy as him.

I can remember a time during my drinking days when my

oldest sister and I were shopping for a video to rent while I was living with my parents and trying to get my teaching certificate. When I applied for the rental card, one of the spaces to fill out was "address." I laughed and asked my sister if I should just put down my car-tag number. We both got a kick out of it, but it was the sickening truth, and I almost felt like I had stepped back in time. I knew my home was with Jim, but I just could not get past the thought of everything I had left behind, especially my very dear friend back in Colorado City. It occurred to me at that very moment that I needed to get back to attending AA meetings. I was sure I was going to be a witch until I got acclimated to my new life; but it was still up to me to choose to either be a happy witch or a miserable witch. After being a long-time member, I knew AA could help me make that distinction.

Jim had a housekeeper that came every other week, which helped, but when all the family was in residence, the house always needed attention. The boys' bathroom needed to be cleaned every day just like the kitchen. I was always loading and unloading the dishwasher and clothes into the washer and dryer. I had talked Jim into letting me take over the laundry; I didn't want him to have to do laundry when he got home, and I wanted my socks to stay white.

Needless to say, I didn't clean the bathroom every day. I wouldn't let the boys use our bathroom; it was off limits except for an emergency. All four had to use the same bathroom and it could get pretty rank. That week, I purposely let it go until I couldn't stand it anymore. Before I attempted to clean the toilet and surrounding area, I decided to pursue an idea.

"Boys, come here!"

Sam, Cooper, Caleb, and Cody came running.

"What?"

"Come into the bathroom."

"What?"

"Close the door."

"Why?"

"Everybody gather around the toilet. Now take a big whiff. Smell the wonderful aroma."

"Peewww."

"Gross."

"Ewww!"

Everyone was in perfect harmony as they expressed their opinion. I would have given anything to have a picture of their faces. I asked if they knew what was causing the bathroom to stink.

Sam spoke up first, "It smells like pee!"

I responded, "That's what it is!" Standing at the door to keep them from running out, I explained that it was because they kept missing the toilet. "Do you think I enjoy cleaning around the toilet?"

I think everyone was in agreement when it came to finding no joy in wiping up pee. I believe they had an eye-opener realization that day when I told them I wasn't going to clean up their messes. I handed everyone a paper towel doused in Lysol and told them to get after it. They looked at me like I had come from outer space. Maybe I had, but as long as we lived in that house, the toilet never smelled as bad as it did that afternoon.

The next chore was to show them how much fun it was to chisel off dried toothpaste where they had spit and not rinsed the sink. Maybe I would do that next time. I certainly didn't want to overwhelm them before I could get them to start hitting the toilet.

* * *

At night, I began working with Cody. What a nightmare! Our battle of wills was truly a control issue. He was convinced he wasn't going to read and I was convinced he would. We sat at the table with flash cards of the alphabet, phonics, and some simple first grade words. He wouldn't even try, and my temper flared. I had very little patience with this child and he knew it. He seemed to think if he just stayed stoic, then I would give up... NOT! I would not back off. I kept thinking of the struggle Cody would have throughout his life if he could not start to read now.

I got within inches from his face and made him look at me. He never looked at anything but the floor, and to make him look me in the eyes seemed painful. I could not understand this little fellow, but it didn't matter. He was going to READ.

"Look at me, Cody!"

He tried but I could see that his facial muscles were straining. He could only look up for just a few seconds before his eyes fell back to the floor.

"LOOK AT ME!"

He tried again, but his gaze fell back to the floor.

With all the sternness that I could muster without losing my temper completely, I told him, "Cody, you're not going to win this one. There is no other option. You are going to learn to read and there is no getting around it. I'm bigger and I'm going to win. You *will* learn to read if it kills us both."

I backed off a bit and said in a gentler voice, "Cody. We are going to sit here night after night, hour after hour until you learn to read and are caught up with your class. The faster you get with the program and cooperate, the less painful it will be for you. I'm telling you, it's going to happen. You are going to read and you will be happy about your accomplishment."

He looked at me and seemed to understand, but at that

time I was not sure of his capabilities. I wasn't sure if he was mentally handicapped, but I was going to give him the benefit of the doubt.

That evening, we made a little progress, but it was tough. Every night for many weeks, we had to get past the control issue. I had to remind him more times than not I was going to win and that he might as well just go along for the ride. Until we got past that standoff each evening, we couldn't get anything accomplished. Once there was that understanding, we made great strides.

Cody and I established a special bond and it wasn't until months later that I realized he was the smartest one of the crop. His reasoning skills were amazing and he could analyze things his brothers couldn't even begin to understand. His school admitted him into some very special programs. He took speech therapy and was allowed to go to content mastery classes. Most importantly, he was learning to read.

His first grade teacher kept telling him to sit up, but his back muscles were too weak. His occupational therapist got him a big rubber ball to sit on and we got one for home, too. We had him sit on it to read, eat, watch television, and play video games. We also took him to therapy sessions outside of school to work on simple motor skills and spatial relationships. Within a short period, Cody began to read, his self-esteem soared sky high, and he realized he was a very special, very bright child. No longer did I have to worry about loving him. Cody and I were an item. Even though it had been very painful for both of us, we established an unbreakable bond.

* * *

Caleb was definitely the people pleaser of the triplets. You know when kids lose their two front teeth? When Caleb lost his, he was so stinking cute! He was by far the most articulate child I have ever known. He tried so hard to pronounce the words correctly, but missing those two front teeth made it nearly impossible. I loved hearing him talk! One evening, I was in the kitchen concocting one of my delicious meals…or so we thought. Bored from playing with the other C's and Sam, Caleb ventured into my space. In that so innocent and sweet voice with the gap in his front teeth, he snuggled up beside me and said with a lisp, "What's for dinner, Mom?"

First, my heart melted. Any time, one of the triplets called me "Mom" it was an earth shaker. In just a few months I found it comforting that I could be considered "Mom" to them. That was a true sign my vision of becoming a loving blended family was coming to fruition.

Oh, boy! I could not wait to try my imagination on Caleb's question: *What's for dinner?* I had decided again on steak fingers, mashed potatoes with gravy, and corn on the cob. Wait! What? I had forgotten to take into account Caleb being toothless. I was ashamed of myself, to say the least.

I bent down next to that precious boy. "Caleb, we are having steak fingers and mashed potatoes, but for you, it is also something very special! You will have to find out the surprise at dinner."

He gave me a hug and skipped, yes *skipped* away. You see, this was all going to work. Maybe.

"Boys! Wash up! Time for dinner!"

Caleb's plate was special. Instead of the regular meal, I made Caleb's look like a rocket. The corn cob was the rocket, held up by the mashed potatoes, and the gravy was the steam when the fuel ignited.

The boys ran to the table, and Caleb's face lit up. As they

sat down, I explained, "Gentlemen, tonight is very special. One of you is being honored for having no front teeth."

I tried as hard as I could to hold a straight face as I approached Caleb's rocket with the biggest butcher knife I could find. As I sliced the corn off of Caleb's cob, I tried to explain to the others the benefit of having teeth. Ha!

They all giggled furiously, and I felt Jim's laughter within mine.

I was trying very hard not to smile as I held up a butcher knife and said, "God loves all people including those with no teeth." More laughter. I said, "Let us pray."

Surprisingly, all the children were still and quiet as Jim prayed, "Dear Lord, thank you for my family and thank you for this food. Amen." He knew from experience to keep it short.

That was Cooper and Cody's first time to attempt to eat corn on the cob. As you probably guessed, it was not successful.

After the corn-rocket dinner, Caleb gave me the warmest hug. He then took a step back, looked me in the eye, and with that ever so delightful attempt at making proper phonics with no front teeth, said, "I love you, Mom."

WOO HOO!

*　*　*

As you can probably imagine, laundry was unimaginable. With triplets, I had expected their clothes to match and all be the same size. That wasn't at all the case in this family. Cody was pencil thin and Caleb ran a close second. Cooper was a little bigger and not so thin. The parents wrote their names on the inside of their clothes, mostly on the labels. And do not forget, we could not use initials here; they were the same!

One week I was doing laundry on a Saturday, and sorting

underwear and socks. Socks were a no brainer. Every triplet had about the same size foot, so I just pitched a half dozen into each triplet's cubbyhole. There was the right number of underwear for Caleb and Cody, but Cooper kept coming up short. As a matter of fact, there was not one pair of underwear in the dirty clothes for Cooper. *What is up with that?* I wondered.

I was putting clothes away and called Cooper to meet me in his bedroom. Thank goodness they were all pretty good about coming to me when I called their name.

"Yes, Mom? Whatcha need?" He looked so terribly innocent.

I said, "Cooper, I was doing laundry and noticed you did not have any underwear in the dirty clothes. Are you out? Do you have any underwear at all?"

His face got as white as a ghost, and he suddenly looked scared. He kept his eyes locked on me but didn't say a word. I was so confused. Was he eating his underwear because I was starving him at mealtime? Surely not.

"Cooper," I repeated. "Where is all your underwear?"

He continued to stare and still did not speak.

"It's okay, Cooper. No matter what you tell me, you won't be in trouble. Just tell the truth, please." His deadpan stare didn't waver. I sat down on the bed and pulled him to me. "What is it, Cooper? Please tell me!"

He then moved toward his closet. At the back corner was all of his clean underwear. "They are all here, Mom."

Oh, my goodness! All clean underwear. "Are you not wearing any underwear each day?"

In a shaky voice, he answered, "I wear the same underwear every day."

"Really? Why in the world?" Oh, boy! I could not wait to hear his explanation.

In a very sweet voice, he said, "I heard you complaining

about all the underwear. How you had to look at each label to see who's underwear belonged to who before putting it away. I thought you wouldn't have to work so hard if you didn't have to sort mine."

Oh, my word! I melted. This moment seemed like a fairytale. Not real. I got down on my knees and pulled Cooper into my arms. "You are so sweet!" I released him and looked him in the eye. "Cooper, you are very special. As a matter of fact, you are so special, I do not want you to wear the same underwear every day!" I explained to him that a few more pieces of laundry would be manageable, and in the future, I could use his help sorting socks. I told him he needed to get clean underwear every day; this was absolutely a necessity.

I gave him a hug and told him how much I loved him. He hugged me back and kissed me on the cheek. "I love you, too, Mom." He smiled as he left the room.

I sighed with happy relief. Cooper and I were going to be okay.

Eleven

Almost exactly one month after Jim and I were married, he came home with a bit of information that was devastating to my simple mind. He informed me that the triplets' mom was taking a job in Abilene, over a 160 miles away, and we would be getting full custody starting in February.

What? I didn't think I was hearing this right. *You mean the triplets will be living here full-time, 24/7 for Jim and I to rear?* I was livid when I heard this news, because as a stay-at-home mom, it would mostly be me doing the rearing.

Jim and I needed some space from parenting four boys to start our new life as a couple. This couldn't be happening. I wanted to wake up and discover this was only a nightmare. But I was already awake and this was a reality gone badly.

Jim assured me everything would be fine, and we would survive. The boys would visit their mother every other weekend and that would give me a break. Somehow, every other weekend didn't seem like enough, but Jim's voice was so soothing. He told me we would get someone to keep the kids on some of the weekends, and he and I would take some romantic getaways. Also, he told me their mother would be paying child support.

My head was spinning. Was there anything I could do about the situation? Since Jim was managing conservator of the triplets, there wasn't anything I could do to change the deal except take Sam and walk away from this marriage. I wasn't ready to do that because I was still thinking of how wonderful life was going to be married to this man. I also loved him very much. I remembered something I learned in AA: nothing is permanent. Okay. Let me think about this. It might not be that bad.

Child support to help with the groceries, clothes, bills, and occasional weekends away with the man I loved, plus a guaranteed weekend off every other weekend were all advantages to this new development. Then I heard this little voice from ages ago saying, "You can do it." This was going to be a challenge but the more I thought about it, the more I began to feel okay.

The most important factor was how this move was going to impact the triplets. I knew they loved their mother fiercely and would miss her. On the other hand, their lives would begin to have some consistency and stability. The house rules between homes were totally different and if they could stay in one place for a period of time and become adjusted to a new way of life (my way, of course!), life would be easier for everyone concerned.

* * *

Days after learning about this monumental responsibility of parenting the triplets fulltime, I was still a raving maniac. I desperately needed an AA meeting.

Okay, I thought, taking in a deep breath, *maybe this is God's plan*. I tried hard to think positive and make sense of this whole thing. I knew in my heart that one home would be best for the boys, because every time they moved in and out on Sunday nights, it was a big adjustment for everyone. For days, Sam moped around and didn't enjoy school when the

Three C's were gone. When they lived at home, everyone but me seemed happier. I was nothing but a grouch. My temperament kept getting worse; I needed some professional help and a regular check-up, too.

I got a referral for a doctor and set an appointment. I told Dr. Kim about my predicament, gave her some of my symptoms, and the testing began. After giving blood and receiving the results, I went back to her office for a consultation. I learned I was anemic, hypoglycemic, and my hormone levels were low. She was amazed I was still functioning. She prescribed iron and estrogen, gave me some dietetic guidelines for low blood sugar and put me on a mild anti-depressant.

Thank goodness for Dr. Kim. She probably kept me from killing someone, because six weeks passed before the triplets left for that "every other weekend" visit to Abilene. In the meantime, I had learned that Jim had filed bankruptcy a few years back, and now had credit card debt of over $10,000! What was I thinking? I should have found out more about my beloved and his banking habits before I said, "I do."

Jim was always so smooth when it came to talking about finances. He would say, "We can manage." Now, I understood what "manage" meant to him. *Put it on a credit card! We can pay it off later.*

Once again, my head was spinning. I immediately recognized those "romantic getaways" were not going to happen. I was a stepmom to triplets married to a poor lawyer. I had left my nice cozy life in Colorado City for this?

Wait a minute. I loved this man. I said "I do" because I had fallen head over heels in love with him. I had married him for better or for worse and had made a vow to stay with him as long as we both shall live. I felt overwhelmed by all my challenges, but I was going to make this work. So I dug my heels in and worked harder than ever to save money and pay off those credit cards. I was still thinking about that new house and I didn't want old debts standing in our way.

* * *

The next six weeks was definitely a test for all of us. One day the school nurse called and it appeared one of the boys had chicken pox. *NO!* It did not take long to estimate either one or two boys would be home, in my space all day, out of school for at least a month, maybe more. There would not be any down-time or time alone to regroup. I would go nuts.

I never knew how hard it would be to plan a weekly menu for six people, especially with very fussy eaters. It also seemed I was on their case for everything: not eating their vegetables, talking with their mouths full and not holding their forks right. I was always giving orders, demanding re-dos or refereeing. To add to my struggles, around this time, I noticed that Jim was enjoying his bourbon a little too much.

About the time we got through the chicken pox, one of the boys brought home a nasty little intestinal flu germ from school. Of course, it made its rounds through the household, and as everyone else was getting well, it hit me. One morning I had to nudge Jim and tell him he would have to do all the morning duties. I was bedridden all day. Like a champion, he took control and managed the day without me.

When I got a note from school and found out how the germ was transferred from body to body, I was livid. Imme-diately I taped a big, bold sign above the toilet in the boys' bathroom: WASH YOUR HANDS!

I had gradually weaned the boys from having to be led out of the school. Now, they walked all the way to the van from their classrooms, and I had Sam leading the way. When it got warmer, I even coerced them into walking one and a half blocks from the school to the house. The home was deadly silent until they hit the backdoor. Then, backpacks were flying, notes shoved in my face and everyone tried to tell me something at the same time.

Once they calmed down, we would start on homework. Even though the Three C's had different teachers, they almost always had the same homework. Caleb and Cooper would finish in about five minutes, but Cody and I were usually the last ones at the table. He still moved very slow, but his work was consistently good and getting better. After all the homework was done, I started dinner.

Almost every day when Jim got home, I was in a bad mood. I was a witch and I knew it, but I really didn't care. I kept trying to do the impossible and I behaved like a typical dry drunk. I was miserable and wanted everyone else to be miserable, too. Jim would go to the liquor cabinet and poor himself a stiff drink. Looking back, I understand why he wanted to escape, but it was not okay with me. He drank until bedtime and then usually went straight to sleep. I could not see how someone could drink that much and still get up at 4:00 in the morning to hold court. This man was amazing.

But, this wasn't working. I felt very jealous that he could escape through the liquor and all I had was a measly anti-depressant. It wasn't fair! I sat down with him one evening between homework and dinner and asked him if he was having trouble dealing with me and the kids. He asked why, and I pointed out his liquor indulgence. I told him if that was the problem, something was going to have to change. The kids would have to go, I would go, or he would have to stop drinking every night. I could not live like this.

He was very understanding and agreed it wasn't fair. He admitted that the total change of his life was a little hard to deal with, and he was finding comfort in the alcohol. We agreed the whole thing had been very difficult for everyone, but I wasn't helping matters either. I was acting like a spoiled brat, he was drinking more, and then I resented the fact that he was escaping. We were caught in a vicious cycle and something had to give. I promised to be more pleasant. He agreed to quit drinking during the week. We sealed the deal with a kiss and a promise, and we were determined to make this work.

* * *

The triplets' mom finally called and said she could take the boys for a weekend. *Hallelujah!*

The weekend they went to their mom's, we took a long hard look at a new house, started checking out some plans, and invited Kay and Terry over for dinner. Terry was the home-builder who had agreed to help us build our new house. This was exciting! We piled into the car after dinner and headed to a division where Terry had just built a new home. We picked a lot we wanted to build on, right across the alley from Terry and Kay.

What a deal! I thought. *Let's get this thing rolling.*

Finding plans to build a house was not a piece of cake. We couldn't afford more than about 2,000 square feet, and Jim wanted a basement for safety reasons. He claimed if the weather was bad, he wanted a place where we could all hibernate, go to sleep, and not worry about tornadoes. We couldn't find a plan less than 3,000 square feet with five bedrooms. They just didn't exist. When the triplets were at school, I started working up some plans of my own.

Aunt Mollie and her husband had drawn up their own plans and had built about eleven homes from scratch. I knew she could help. She and I, with the help of a scanner and the internet, worked on a plan for months. I would take it to the draftsman, and usually it was over 3,000 square feet. At one point, the living room was only about seven feet wide, and another time, the plans came back to me without a shower in the master bathroom.

Jim and I both wanted a snail shower, without a door, and Terry said it was nearly impossible. *Don't tell me it's impossible!* I worked the snail shower into the bathroom and on graph paper it looked great, but apparently, the draftsman didn't want to include it, or the tile man didn't want to build it. Regardless of the reason, our snail shower had gotten nixed. Back to square one.

About three months had passed and I still hadn't come up with an acceptable plan. Both Aunt Mollie and I were very frustrated. What to do? One morning, after taking the kids to school, it was cold and I had a fire going with the plans laid out on the coffee table. I got down on my knees and prayed. All else had failed, so why not?

I prayed to God to show me the way. I prayed for His will and I prayed for His guidance to help me draw house plans that would work. I knew if He wanted us to have a new house, then only He could help. When I got up, I went to the plans, erased a few lines, re-drew, and in thirty minutes, I was on my way to the draftsman to get him to draw up the plans from the new sketch.

It worked! Isn't it amazing how we can forget to ask God for help until all else has failed? The plans ended up being just a little over 2,000 square feet and they were doable. Terry approved the plans and our dream home was about to come into existence. I knew it was going to take more time and effort before we could move in, but at least we were on our way. I have no doubts that I would still be working on those plans today, if I hadn't sought God's help. I will never forget that day, that miracle, and that valuable lesson.

We were on our way to having a beautiful new home. We had designed it especially for our family. The boys' wing was on the west side with a basement for a game room, and our wing was on the east side, separated by the family room and a huge kitchen and dining area. There would be enough room to feed eighteen people at the same time, in the same room. With a stroke of genius, I even planned separate heating and cooling units for the east side and west side. With so much testosterone running rampantly in the teenage years, Jim and I would need our own air.

The spacious kitchen was going to be wonderful. All the boys could line up on stools at the island, and with two microwaves, breakfast would materialize in about three minutes. And with two dishwashers, cleaning up would be faster too. In the old house, frustration heightened when all the dishes were in the dishwasher and still dirty. That was not going to happen anymore.

Jim and I were so excited. Terry was ready to buy the lot and get things rolling. He told us construction could be finished in about six months. We would be moving into our new home around Christmas, and with this news, I figured I could handle managing this family and get to the point where I wanted to be. Now I was going to be married to an attorney, living in the big city, and enjoying a fabulous new home. Things were really looking up despite the fact that I had four little boys underfoot!

PART THREE

A Twist of Fate
and
Test of Faith

Twelve

Jim received an offer to go to a seminar in Austin, and asked if I wanted to go and bring the boys with us. They would have to miss a few days of school, but I was game. We could stay at the hotel during the day and play in the pool, and Uncle Dee and Aunt Mollie lived nearby. I was ecstatic. I wanted them to visit with the triplets. This was going to be great!

We got adjoining rooms. The boys loved the white bath robes and Sam loved the free coffee. Everything worked well. We went to visit my aunt and uncle, and the triplets behaved very well. Aunt Mollie and Uncle Dee acknowledged I was making a difference.

On the drive home, something very strange happened. Since I had been to visit regularly, I knew the roads like the back of my hand. We were all loaded up, and I told Jim where to go and when we would make an exit.

As we were heading down I-35, I said, "Take the next exit." He said, "Okay."

At that time, one of the triplets started complaining, and I turned around to see if I could help. Jim flew right past the exit.

"What? I told you to exit!" I was not very complacent when it came to people not considering my directions. I unleashed my anger on him. "Why didn't you exit back there?"

He just kept a stiff upper lip and refused to answer.

After about fifteen minutes, we got back on the right track, and I calmed down. However, I still could not understand why he completely ignored me.

Later one night, we had Jon and Derek over for dinner and were telling them about all the problems we had stumbled over trying to draw up the plans for the new house. Jim shared stories of taking the plans time after time to the drafter and getting rejections time after time. He told the boys about the time we got the plans back and there was no shower in the master bathroom. This was very normal; Jim was a great storyteller. However, in five minutes, he started telling the story all over again, using exactly the same words, the same way, as if he had never told it before.

What was happening? Maybe I was having some kind of *déjà vu* experience and only thought I had already heard Jim telling that story. I was confused and looked at Derek and Jon. Derek looked a little strange, but Jim continued talking, then the story passed, and no one said anything.

Jim had been having a few headaches, lately, too. I just discounted them, saying they were probably sinus headaches caused by allergies. We got him some high-powered allergy medicine, and there was always plenty of Ibuprofen in the cabinet. Thinking back, now I remember Jim would ask for four Ibuprofen at a time for relief for his headaches.

At night, while lying in bed together, it was usual practice for us to say we loved each other with a kiss. After all, we had only been married about six months, and I was determined that the honeymoon was still on.

One particular night Jim said, "I love you, Lynette."

"I love you, too, Jim."

Then we both said, "Goodnight."

Then he said again, "I love you, Lynette."

"I love you, too. Goodnight."

"Goodnight."

Seconds later… "I love you, Lynette."

"I love you." One more time? No! In actuality, this went on about eight times before I asked Jim if he realized what he was doing. My heart started beating fast and I was scared. He got a little defensive and asked if it was a problem if he wanted to say he loved me. *No, no problem.* I just wanted to find out if Jim knew what he was doing. He let out a very heavy sigh, and I could hear a distinct difference in his voice. He was actually trying very hard not to start crying.

He began to talk about some incidences he had experienced at the university. He had ventured out of the office several times, arriving at another building on campus, then once getting there, he had forgotten why he had gone. He talked about the secretaries at work asking, "Don't you remember?" too often, and he described some occurrences he'd had while driving. Several times, he had been on his way to work or on his way back home and not known where he was or where he was going. He said those moments would only last a few minutes, but nonetheless, those moments frightened him.

Why was this happening? We both tried to come up with some reasons. Maybe he had a virus in his head. Maybe the lining of his brain was swelling and causing problems with his thinking. Or maybe he had a sinus infection and instead of messing with his equilibrium, it was messing with his thought process. No, wait! It suddenly became clear. It was just stress. A new wife had completely changed Jim's life, and he had never had to deal with having four boys around 24/7. If we could relieve his stress, everything would be fine.

But how? I had already rearranged everything but the structure of the house. I had completely reorganized the kitchen cabinets. Nothing was familiar in the garage. And his closets had been invaded. The only thing that was really his anymore was the top underwear drawer of his dresser. His toothbrush still remained in the same place but everything else at home had changed, including his vehicle. The van suited transportation needs of the children, so Jim was driving the sedan.

I set up an appointment with our primary care doctor, and Jim and I went together the very next day. I wanted to make sure the doctor got all the information Jim had relayed to me. You know, sometimes men are funny. They put off going to the doctor until they cannot get out of bed, and then when the doctor comes in the examination room, everything is fine.

"How are you?"

"Fine, doctor. Just fine."

The doctor ordered a bunch of tests and wanted Jim to go for an MRI that afternoon. Of course, she was unable to get him in that soon, so they scheduled one for the next morning. I wanted to go, but Jim convinced me that he could handle it.

"Okay, go," I said. "I will see you after work. Have a good day and let me know how it goes."

It was summertime and the triplets were out of school. I had enrolled them in vacation Bible school, which kept them busy in the mornings. The last day was Friday. Jim had gone for his MRI on Thursday. The doctor's office set up an appointment for 1:00 Monday to discuss the test results.

We have to wait until Monday to find out? I was ready to know now.

Since Friday morning was the last day of vacation Bible school, the triplets were going to sing in a finale. At 11:00 a.m., Jim met us at the church and together we sat down to watch the program. I had left my cell phone in the van, but Jim's went off about 11:45.

After he finished taking the call, I asked, "What's up?"

"The doctor wanted to change the appointment to this afternoon."

I became filled with concern. "Why did they move it to today?"

He shrugged his shoulders and we finished watching the boys in their debut.

Afterward, Jim and I kissed goodbye, and the boys loaded up in the van to go home. My cell phone beeped that I had a message waiting. I did not pay much attention, but the phone number looked strangely familiar. When I realized it was the doctor's office, I stopped dead in my tracks. Something was wrong. All kinds of thoughts went through my head. Uncontrollable thoughts that I did not want to face. My hands trembled as I punched in the number. The receptionist answered, I told her who I was, and she proceeded to tell me they needed both Jim and I to come to the office that afternoon.

This was bad. Very bad.

What about the triplets? They were out of school and I needed someone to watch them. I thought of Dennie and Dave. Dennie only worked part time, and since Dave was retired, they were free to watch the boys. I dropped them off on the way to the doctor's.

Dave met us in the driveway and noticed my concern. He said, "It will be okay, and don't you worry about the boys. They'll be fine."

I knew they would be, but what about Jim? My stomach churned as I drove the van to the doctor's. We arrived almost at the same time. Jim was getting out of the car when I pulled into the parking lot. He smiled, but there was no twinkle in his eyes anymore. I could read his face: he was concerned too. We clutched each other's hands and headed toward the door. It was not long before they called his name, and we were ushered to a small examination room.

Jim's primary care doctor had quit seeing regular patients; so when we talked about seeing a doctor, the suggestion was to see the same one who had helped with all my issues. She was very young, but very adequate; and she had a professionalism about her that impressed us both. She had fixed me, and now she would fix Jim.

After a few moments of chitchat between us, she whirled in the door. "Good afternoon! Good to see you."

We exchanged smiles and niceties, and then we all sat down to talk shop. She had Jim's chart in her hand and was clenching the metal backing just a little too hard. She began going over the blood work: cholesterol was good, blood sugar in check, protein levels acceptable.

Okay, okay, I thought. *Get on with it.*

Jim and I were nodding our heads. "That's good. Sounds great."

Then she became serious and began, "However, the MRI showed some type of mass."

At that very second, I stopped listening. A mass in Jim's head. That is what she said. What kind of mass? How big is this mass? A tumor? A virus? What is she saying? I tried to pull myself back into the conversation, but I had missed too much. Now, she was saying Jim needed to go to the hospital immediately. She would schedule a biopsy, but she wanted him to remain in the hospital over the weekend for observation.

Now? You are going to take Jim, now?

The doctor ordered a wheelchair.

My head was reeling. This absolutely cannot be happening. What am I going to do with the boys?

I had never had the boys alone for a whole weekend and I was quite sure I would not be able to handle it. I couldn't even handle what was happening at that very moment.

Okay. Get your wits together.

The hospital was attached to the medical building and it wasn't long before we were wheeling Jim down a very long hallway. Cold, white walls. I felt as if we were leaving one world and entering another. The intern pushing Jim did not say a word. Jim's face matched the pale walls. He looked like he might pass out.

I asked, "Are you okay?"

"I'm fine," he said.

Fine. It was the answer everyone gave when their world was caving in, or when they were about to lose their sanity. It was the answer I had always given my family back when I struggled with alcoholism. Many times I had wanted to say, "None of your business," but saying "I'm fine" was just another nicety. I always wondered if they had really wanted to know the truth.

Walking down that hallway allowed too much time to get lost in a storm of bad thoughts. I do not remember the admission process. I do not remember getting Jim to his room, helping him get undressed, or tucking him into that horrible hospital bed. I just went through the motions and didn't even realize what was happening. All of the sudden, I realized we had two cars at the medical building. I quickly called Derek to see if he could come get the car, find a friend to follow him, and take it home. Thank goodness, he was available.

While Jim and I were waiting, we talked about the weekend, arrangements for the boys, and whether or not I needed to be there at the hospital. Observation. That was all it was. The doctor wanted him to remain in the hospital for observation. I could probably stay with the kids; no, I would have to. Jim would be fine at the hospital, because, after all, a hospital is swarming with caregivers. Derek would take the car; I would pick up the triplets and go home. Derek could stay with the triplets until I packed a bag for Jim and brought it to the hospital. Okay. Everything is going to be fine. Fine. There was that word again.

In a few minutes, Derek arrived. Once again, we were speaking all those niceties. I was beginning to hate niceties. I kissed Jim goodbye, told him I would be back as soon as possible, and then Derek and I walked out the door. At that moment, the floods came.

Overwhelmed with fear, I could not stop crying. I wept in the elevator in my son's arms and it was awkward. He had never seen his mother this way. He did not know what to say or do. He patted and tried to soothe me, saying he was sure everything would be fine. That blasted word again! My new, safe world was crumbling around me, like a dry piece of cake that had been saved one too many days without any cover.

Thirteen

When I arrived back at the hospital with Jim's overnight bag, the neurosurgeon was in his room. Again, niceties. Good to meet you...not. I could think of a hundred other people I would have been happy to meet other than a neurosurgeon. First, any doctor seemed intimidating. Second, his presence was a reminder of why we were meeting a brain surgeon at this particular time.

Jim was fully dressed and out of bed. What was going on? The doctor seemed terribly young, but serious about the situation. With an air of knowledge and wisdom, along with so-so bedside manners, he explained the situation. I tried with all my might to soak in the information he was spilling forth. I had to make a conscientious effort to pay attention, because my mind kept wandering off to a place it would rather be.

The doctor explained there was no reason for Jim to stay in the hospital over the weekend. With this sort of tumor, seizures were very rare, but he was prescribing anti-seizure medication just in case.

Wait! Jim had a *tumor*? We thought it was just a mass! What did this mean? Wait, Dr. Whatever-your-name-is, what do you mean "a tumor"?

I could not ask the question and Dr. Wills just kept talking. I did not have a clue what he was saying. All I could think about was a tumor in Jim's head. What did this mean? This was truly a nightmare. We had just gotten married and we had our entire lives before us. People with brain tumors die!

As the doctor was writing out the prescription, I tried to listen to what he was saying. We could stop at the pharmacy on the way home. Dr. Wills explained he was scheduling a biopsy for the following Tuesday. We could come to the hospital on Monday for all the pre-admission requirements so we would be ready for the procedure on Tuesday morning.

I vaguely remember asking the doctor to explain the procedure. Jim would be under a general anesthesia. After drilling a hole in Jim's skull, the doctor would guide a needle through his brain using a computerized program created from the MRI.

What were the possible side effects of such a radical intrusion of the delicate brain tissue? There were risks, of course. Swelling was the worst, and there was always a chance of infection. What would happen in the case of swelling?

I took a deep breath. My stomach started churning as I listened to the doctor tell us about all the possible side effects. Swelling in the brain could cause the inability to think straight, inability to form words, loss of mobility, loss of sight, impaired hearing; the list went on and on.

We do not want to do this! I wanted to say.

The doctor went on to say these side effects were very rare. The procedure was simple and calculated, and in most cases, it would not affect the delicate brain tissue. Later, we would see the full-blown effects of such an evil, ugly organism living in Jim's brain.

The neurosurgeon explained this was a necessary procedure. He wanted to make sure the tumor was what he expected. The doctors needed to know what kind of tumor they were dealing with before they could formulate a treatment plan.

I was shaking as I said, "Treatment plan? What kind of

treatment plan?"

The doctor's answer was "Chemotherapy and radiation."

My voice trembled and my knees turned weak. "You mean Jim has cancer?" This simply was not possible. I was thinking that I might not like this doctor very much at all.

The doctor's eyes softened. I knew then how hard it must be to be a doctor. To tell people horrible things and supply them with facts they did not want to know would have to be the hardest job on the face of this earth. To struggle with compassion and to maintain a professional attitude must be the ultimate clash of a lifetime. Earlier in Dr. Kim's office, these things did not cross my mind. Now, as I saw this doctor trying to be empathetic and businesslike at the same time, I understood what Dr. Kim must have gone through, too. No one wants to tell a person he has a brain tumor and it does not look good. Life is so hard sometimes...especially when you get unimaginable news, or if you happen to be a doctor or a neurosurgeon. At that point, I had compassion for both Dr. Kim and Dr. Wills.

After a few seconds passed since I had asked if Jim had cancer, Dr. Wills said, "I'm afraid so, but that's why we must take a biopsy. We want to be sure."

Since the hospital had admitted Jim, we had to wait for a wheelchair. The wait seemed discomfited, and the broken moments of silence were uncomfortable. The doctor did his best to wish us a good weekend, but the effort seemed lame. Yeah, right. You just told us Jim has a cancerous brain tumor, and you want us to have a good weekend. As the wheelchair arrived, the neurosurgeon paused at the door on his way out and said to Jim and I, "Try to relax over the next few days, and I'll see you on Tuesday." He was going to have a good weekend, I could tell. This was not fair!

Jim rode home with Derek, and I headed to Dave and

Dennie's to pick up the boys. When I got there, they were playing football in the front yard with Dave. Dennie was sitting in a chair on the porch. I told the boys to get in the van. Then I broke the bad news with Dennie and Dave. They were as devastated as I was. They had been friends with Jim for a very long time.

The boys, unaware of what was happening, were their normal boisterous selves, while Jim and I remained in a daze for the rest of the evening. We did not say much to each other. With the boys, there was always plenty to do, and if we ever found a quiet moment, one of them needed something or we had to resolve a conflict. There was not a lot of time for thought, so bedtime was a welcome event. I wanted to talk to my husband alone. With dinner done, baths taken, prayers said, all the boys were in bed by 10:00 and it was time for us. It had been a long day.

We just held each other that night. Jim did not say a word. I tried to get him to talk but all he could do was cry. He said he was scared. So was I. I prayed aloud for both of us, prayed for guidance and the strength to see this through. This was a nightmare and we wanted it to go away. Deep down, both of us knew it was not going away.

* * *

The next day was a normal Saturday, considering the bombshell news we had received the day before. Jim was sullen, but once again, with the boys around, there was not much time for self-pity or grief. Since Dave and Dennie knew about the mass in Jim's head, they had contacted our pastor and several of our closest friends. Soon, the phone started ringing and people wanted to let us know about their concerns.

Kathryn, our pastor, had become a close friend of mine.

Before the wedding, we had met at the church the day I lost my voice. After a few phone chats and learning we were both runners, Kathryn and I became running partners and fast friends. She called that day and wanted to know if it would be okay to tell the congregation about Jim's diagnosis on Sunday. Of course, it was okay. It was more than okay because the more people who knew about the tumor, the more people we would have praying for us. We would need all the prayers we could get. We elected not to go to church that particular Sunday.

Terry had called for some other reason, but after I told him about the tumor, I suggested holding off the closing on the lot for the house. I did not know what our plans were, or what we should do; we needed some time to sort things out and construct a plan. How we would do just that was a mystery to us both. Muddy waters made it impossible to have any clear thoughts, and the notion of a cancerous tumor destroyed any attempts to formulate a plan.

Sunday evening finally came, and Jim and I had to talk. We had to get this out in the open. Jim had said very little throughout the weekend, and now it was time for some discussion. I cornered him in the bedroom as he was exiting the master bath. I shut the door, hoping for a little privacy before dinner.

I said, "We need to talk."

His eyes were blank and his lips became taut.

"Jim, we have to talk about some things and make some decisions. We cannot just pretend Friday did not happen."

With a defensive tone he said, "What do you want me to say?"

There was a cold tension in the air and I hesitated. Then I asked, "Do you think you are the only one this is happening to?"

He glared and did not utter a word.

"Do you think you are the only one affected by the news we got on Friday?" I exploded. "You are selfish if you think I am not hurting, too! Do you think I am not devastated as well? Your job is easy. All you have to do is die! I will be the one left behind expected to put all the pieces back together!"

I could not believe the words coming out of my mouth. Cruelness was not my intention, but no one ever knows how emotions are going to affect our verbal communication.

When I stopped yelling and stared at Jim, there was a look of awe on his face. "Do you think I'm going to die?"

Tears welled up in my eyes. "I do not know! Do *you* think you are going to die?"

He said he had been thinking about it all weekend, and he was aware there was a very big possibility. We agreed neither knew what the future would bring, but we were willing to put up a big fight and do everything humanly possible to get rid of the cancer. He said he wanted to fight, he wanted to live, and we made a pact at that moment to keep the possibility of death out of our conversations. We were both crying by the time we stopped talking. We decided to go on and build the house. We were going to live for the future and not wait around for death.

* * *

Jim called Terry and told him to continue with the plans to close on the lot and break ground. Could we do this? Would any mortgage company in their right mind grant a loan to a client diagnosed with a brain tumor? Terry said we could do it. He knew people in the business who would help us get the funding. This was just another Godsend.

Next, Jim called Jon and Josh to break the news, but his voice was jovial, and he kept it light. On the other hand, my family received the news by email. I did not have the guts to talk to them on the phone. I knew I wouldn't be able to hold it together. I heard from most of them right away, but it was not until days later that I heard from one of my sisters. Caye had told Aunt Mollie that she could not call until she could stop crying.

More than anything, the triplets and Sam needed their dad. What would become of their future? Sam and I needed Jim. After battling alcoholism, I needed a good husband. After losing his father, Sam needed Jim to be his dad. I had left my old life with massive faith that this new one was going to be wonderful. Where was God and why had He let this happen? Over the next several months, this question would come up a thousand times. Our situation certainly was not fair, and there was no logical answer. I knew I would have to rely on the principles of AA and my faith as a Christian to get through this horrendous ordeal.

I had been attending AA meetings not far from our house for about three months. When I was losing my mind and found out I was in bad health, I had decided it was time to find a support group. AA seemed like the logical solution, and as always, the fellowship and stability there at the meetings helped sustain the mandatory sobriety and sanity the situation demanded. I had painted a pretty picture to all the members… meeting Jim online, and marrying the man with triplets. I could not bear the thought of facing them now and telling them the dreadful news. Isn't it odd how we push people away when we need them the most?

* * *

Monday morning came and, as usual, Kathryn showed up for our early morning run. Kathryn was another Godsend. This woman truly had God in her heart, and I could feel it.

She was beautiful, a little younger than me, with radiant skin and curly, light brown hair. After jogging for miles and having deep, heartfelt conversations about our blended family and battling the situation, she would come inside and pray with Jim and me. We would hold hands, be still, and witness the spirit within us. Every morning, she assured us that faith and trusting the Lord was the only way we would make it through this terrifying and horrible ordeal.

Have you ever heard of the power of prayer? We will never know how much of an impact Kathryn's presence and her spirituality had on our family, but life would have been much tougher without those few calming and reassuring words every morning. She helped us keep the faith; she helped us stay connected; and above all, she was a true friend. She could always help me laugh and let me cry when I could not laugh anymore.

Somehow, we made it through the biopsy and Jim did not develop any harmful side effects. However, the waiting was unbearable. The biopsy had taken place Tuesday afternoon, and we still had not received the results. What was going on? Why couldn't they tell us anything? Jim had the notion he could sit at home waiting on the results as well as he could lay in the hospital, so in his very diplomatic way, he let the nurse know that he was going home that afternoon. I loved him so very much at that moment. He wanted to spend time with his family, and I desperately needed him nearby. It sounded like a swell plan to me.

It had only been two days, but shuffling between home and the hospital and finding help to stay with the boys had gotten a little old. When Jim said he was going to get his walking papers, I scooted out to get some errands done while the kids were still in school and Jim was still in the hospital. I had not been gone more than twenty minutes when my cell phone rang.

The young neurosurgeon said, "Jim wants to go home."

Duh. I knew that. Apparently, the nurse had called the doctor when Jim expressed his desire to go home, and the doctor dropped what he was doing and made a beeline to Jim's room. He wanted Jim to stay in the hospital until the oncologist could evaluate the situation and construct a treatment plan, but then saw no need to keep him since Dr. Wills could see Jim was all alone and seemed very depressed.

That hurt. I had just left Jim! Did he forget I had been there almost the whole time? And wouldn't you know, the minute I stepped out, the doctor appeared. It is a mystery how we can wait on doctors for hours, then when we least expect them, they appear like magic. It took all I could muster to not let my alligator mouth overload my hummingbird butt again, but I maintained and listened to what he had to say. I will never forget his words.

"The mass in Jim's head is a glioblastoma tumor. It is cancerous, very aggressive and with chemotherapy and radiation, we could sustain his life for eighteen to twenty months."

The devastating news buckled my knees.

My trembling hand could barely hold the phone, as I asked, "What would happen if we elected not to go through the treatment process?"

He paused, as if he didn't want to answer. Very gently, he said, "He will be gone in three, maybe four months." I really began to hate this doctor.

During admissions for the biopsy, we had read some very hopeful information. On one of the forms, a paragraph led us to believe the same needle used for the biopsy could extract the tumor in the same procedure. We had been ecstatic. We figured the needle could just suck that tumor right out of Jim's head. Before surgery, Dr. Wills had made it clear there was no possibility of that happening. Then after surgery when he found me in the waiting room, he had said the diagnosis was very bad. I had begun to dislike him then, but now, after learning that Jim would die within the next twenty months, I really hated the neurosurgeon.

I asked if Jim knew and the doctor said he had told him. What? He told Jim without me there? I wanted to choke the surgeon. I could not get back to the hospital fast enough. I was dazed with shock and in such denial, but I could not wait to get Jim out of that deathbed and back home where he belonged. I wanted to scream, to cry, to lash out. Nevertheless, I felt numb. I just wanted to get Jim home and hold him forever.

When I got back to the hospital, Jim was dressed and ready to go. We drove home in complete silence. We went through the motions, but there was no life in us. My head felt like a hollow rock and my heart like a glass bowl full of lead beads. I could not think at all anymore...maybe because I did not want to think. I felt as if someone were to bump me, my heart would break and all those little beads would fall to the ground and be lost forever. How could God let this happen?

How do you tell family and friends what is really going on without sounding like you have lost all faith? Jim's diagnosis was dire; no, *terminal*, but how do you actually communicate the worst possible outcome when you are supposed to have faith in God? My struggle with this dilemma became monumental. I was supposed to have faith in God's will, but wasn't it God's will that was going to let my husband die? How in the world do I tell people the truth without sounding as if I have given up all hope? Where was my faith? At that point, I had none. Nil. Nada. Zilch.

I don't know how we got through the next few days; my memory is a blur. It was as if someone had told us that one of us had died, yet we were still both there. We went through a mourning of sorts, but it was abstract, bizarre, morbid, and all encompassing. Every day Death stared us in the face and every breath we took we felt closer to the end. Like a spiraling abyss, it sucked us down, and the path became narrower as we descended into its grip. Death came closer every hour, every day. There was really no way to describe it.

Fourteen

Treatment started immediately. After doing a little research on the internet, I found out the glioma tumor, in stage IV, was rapidly lethal without chemotherapy and radiation. On Monday, we met doctors and scheduled sessions. Jim would start radiation, visiting the cancer center daily for six weeks. After radiation, he would go through chemotherapy.

There went our summer! Their mom was supposed to take the triplets for two weeks that summer, and Jim and I had planned a romantic get-away to be alone for at least one of those weeks. My sister, Caye, had agreed to keep Sam for a week. Jim and I had intended to do something special, but that dream vacation slipped right through our fingers when we opted for the aggressive treatment plan. The words "rapidly lethal" gave us no other option. I remember thinking the timing was bad, but was there ever a good time to get cancer? Obviously, there was never a good time to get terminally ill.

We went to our first session with the doctor in charge of radiation. He was animated and full of optimistic energy. He reminded me of a tall cartoon cowboy, charging forward on his horse, trying to lasso all the little mutated cells. He was not one to give up. When I asked him about Jim and I taking a break for a vacation, the doctor highly discouraged the notion. He said we did not want to give the tumor any time to regroup and gain strength. If we were going to give it the best fight ever, we were going to have to hit the tumor with everything we had. He was ready, armed with his cowboy boots and radiation machine. Even though the proven results showed we could only hope for twenty more months, we believed there was a miracle in store for us. Jim never gave up on that thought… and neither did I.

I could not bear the thought of Jim going to radiation by himself, so in the mornings, he would leave the house early to go on to work, then around 9:00 I would gather up all the boys, load them in the van, and head to Texas Tech to pick Jim up. He would meet us in the parking lot, and we would drive to the cancer center. That is where I found Bobby McMillan.

We had met one Sunday at church when I was visiting Jim before we were married. Bobby had filled in as interim pastor after our church's regular pastor had become ill and before Kathryn had accepted the assignment. Bobby was a retired Methodist preacher and now served as chaplain to the cancer center. What a deal! Another Godsend.

Bobby was a Godly man. He and Kathryn were friends, and I could feel the spirit moving within him like I could feel it in Kathryn. When I saw him, I wanted to be near him, hoping that Godliness would seep into me. If you can imagine, my spirituality had become pretty lame, with Death lurking in the shadows. Somehow, Bobby brought my faith back.

As the boys played in the center's family room, week after week, Bobby patiently listened to my frustration and aggravation of being handed such a rotten deal. He listened as I told him how Jim was withdrawing into his own world and how I felt abandoned. After months of radiation and chemo, Jim had no idea how much this was hurting our relationship. Now, more than ever, I felt like a housekeeper and a nanny. I had already lost my husband without him having one foot in the grave. He would not talk anymore, and his personality had changed dramatically.

Bobby was instrumental in helping me understand and cope with what we were all going through. I will never forget him for the compassion and comfort he gave me that summer.

On top of everything I was dealing with, there were the questions the boys had. Why were we going to this place every day? They did not understand the full grasp of a brain tumor, so I borrowed the MRI pictures from the hospital, taped the film up on the patio doors, sat them down in the front row, and proceeded to explain what that little dot was in the middle of Dad's brain. The boys were very solemn as I explained cancer and how their father had become very ill.

"Is Dad going to die?"

How do you answer that to a seven-year-old boy? They all got very quiet and waited for my response. Their father did not seem sick to them. He was still going to work every day and playing basketball with them in the afternoons. I struggled very hard with some answers. There was that faith issue again. I told them no one but God knew the answer to that question, and we had to have faith God would take care of us and keep us safe.

"If God's supposed to take care of us, why does Dad have this tumor in his brain?"

"Why is he sick?"

I did not know what to say to these precious little boys. I told them we were going to fight the cancer, and we were all going to pray very hard for Dad. We would have to have faith that everything was going to be fine and that God would see us through, no matter what. We needed to help Dad in any way we could, because the radiation and chemotherapy were probably going to take their toll, and soon, Dad would not be feeling very well. I was in tears and could not converse any longer. Can you imagine trying to tell three seven-year-old boys and Jim's new stepson of age eight that their dad was going to die? I skirted the facts. I told them to go play.

In seconds, they scattered. They laughed and played, and one of them asked if we could go swimming. Sure. Why not? The sun would do us all some good and the exercise would help clear my head.

Since Jim was an employee of Texas Tech, we were members of their recreation center (which had a pool), and it was an easy outing. I remember thinking how nice it would have been to be a kid again, and to just push aside reality for an afternoon of swimming and floating down the lazy river.

Those next six weeks were unimaginable. The triplets' mom had not taken them every other weekend as promised. At least while school was in session, I had from 8:00 to 3:00, Monday through Friday, to regroup. Since it was summer, those days were gone and I was fed up with all the kids. All of them, including Sam. I began to get snippy and cross, and was never in a good mood.

I think Sam understood what was happening. He became bossy and controlling. He had already lost his father at the age of three and did not want to lose another one. Sam wanted to be in control. Somehow, he believed if he was in control of the triplets, he could stop the tumor, too. I am a controlling person, also, and I believed if I kept everything in line, kept the family together, kept everything organized, we could beat this tumor and be a whole family.

In many, many ways, I was very blessed that summer. I had complete control...or so I thought. In the mornings, Kathryn, the Saint John's Methodist pastor, was a captive audience during our jog time. At the cancer center, I always had Bobby's attention trying to soothe and calm my frustration, while the boys played in the children's room. Jim stayed active with the boys, but he was helping less and less around the house. Radiation had zapped his strength, his spirits were low, and he was drinking heavily again. Being a recovered alcoholic, I felt resentful, jealous, and angry while still very much in love. I wanted a drink as much as Jim did. However, I knew if I indulged that would be the end of hope for everyone in this very special family.

What could I say? We all wonder how we would act, what we would think, and how we would handle it if we knew we were going to die. Jim used the alcohol as a sedative and a means of escape. I am almost sure I would have done the same thing, if I had known that cancer would just kill me sooner. For alcoholics, to drink is to die, but what if we knew we were going to die anyway?

On several occasions, I tried to talk to Jim and his withdrawal into himself only got worse. He got defensive and said to leave him alone. I was dying inside and once again, I sought out AA. I had turned away from my closest friends when I needed them the most, and now I had to seek their help to get me back on track. After being absent for a while, going back to AA meetings is always humbling, to say the least.

I went to the meetings and explained the situation to my fellow recovering alcoholics, and as usual, they were wonderful. They invited me to call if I needed anything and they supplied me with all kinds of phone numbers and resources. One lady even gave me a book a woman had written when her husband was diagnosed with a brain tumor. There is always strength in numbers, and knowing that someone else had gone through the same ordeal was comforting in a sad, warming way. I had also found a cancer support group who were caregivers, whose spouses were dying, or had already passed. I will always be grateful for the love, care, and support that I found from that group of people. Some of us are still friends.

Fifteen

Our associate pastor at Saint John's Methodist church, Ann, was also a chaplain at one of the hospitals and had stopped to browse in an exclusive clothing store, after having a very trying day. She explained to me later that the store she visited always seemed to cheer her up. That very trying day was the fact that Jim was dying. Ann was also a close friend of Jim's and she had taken the news of Jim very hard.

After browsing a bit and chatting mindlessly, another woman named Michele Ann, who went by "Mike," had sensed that Ann was struggling with a problem. Ann started explaining the situation, and it turned out that Mike had lost her husband two years ago from exactly the same kind of brain tumor. Ann saw an opportunity to bring us together. Ann and Mike were both Godly people, and Ann began to tell Mike about the new woman who had come into Jim's life who was going to be a very good addition to the broken family of Jim and the triplets. Ann told me later that she could physically feel Mike's heart sink when she explained the tumor. Mike wanted to meet me. Ann called me later that day, and insisted Mike and I meet for lunch. I am not very good at meeting new people but I called her anyway and we met at a tea garden.

Mike immediately amazed me. I just knew God had sent me an angel. During lunch, she and I became hard, fast friends.

We just clicked. She had moved to Lubbock a few years back to be near her sister-in-law, but unfortunately the sister-in-law had also been on the internet, married a man, and moved to Marble Falls. Mike lived alone and had no other close family or friends in Lubbock, until she met me. She only worked part time, so she had time for a new friendship. Have you ever heard the phrase "A friend for a reason, a season or a lifetime"? It comes from a poem and the author explained that when someone comes into your life for a particular reason, it is usually to meet a need you or they have prayed for. God had sent Mike to assist our family through difficulty, to provide guidance and support, and to aid us physically, emotionally, and spiritually. The author then goes on to explain that without any wrongdoing, the relationship will come to an end. Sometimes, you just drift apart. Sometimes God will remove them from your life completely. I knew Mike had miraculously appeared for a reason, but I did not want to face the fact that she might not be there for a lifetime. I just felt like I had found a soul mate, and I never wanted our relationship to end. She was gracious, fun, compassionate, and we became best friends.

When we met, she was struggling with trying to find a church home (Baptist), and had not found the right one for her. I talked her into going with us to our church. She had been in music ministry throughout her life; so soon, I had her singing in the choir and playing bells with the adult bell choir. I am surprised I did not have her teaching a Sunday school class, but I guess in all her wisdom, Mike had learned somewhere to say "no." Maybe she could teach me the same lesson.

When it came to Jim or the kids, whenever I needed help with anything, she was Johnny on the Spot. If I needed someone to pick up the boys from school when Jim and I were at the oncologist, Mike would pick them up, take them to the house, and get them rounded at the table to do homework. We would have lunch together often, or meet for coffee in the mornings when Jim was at work and the boys were at school. Mike and I even started a women's club with women from the church who did not work outside of the home. For many months, five of us met on Tuesday mornings, and we called ourselves the Lazy Women's Group. We stayed caught up in each other's lives, gave and took advice freely, laughed heartily, and even cried on occasion. Since then the group has dispersed, but those women were a Godsend, too.

* * *

That summer, Jim maintained his duties as magistrate for the city and continued to work at Texas Tech as the Student Mediation Director, only taking off an hour or so each morning for radiation. Sometimes, he would come home in the afternoon for a short nap only to return to work to maintain his position and his dignity. I know the poor man was exhausted. In addition, he was trying to help me pick out paint, tile, and brick for the new house. We will not mention grout, appliances, cabinet tops, shingles, light fixtures, trim, bathroom fixtures, hardware, doorknobs, or placement of electrical outlets and switches. You should have seen me on the toothpaste aisle at Walmart. I was overwhelmed. I never knew building a house would be so complicated. What was I thinking?

Life was a whirlwind. I tried to teach the boys new life skills (how to spit toothpaste into the water flow to see it disappear down the drain), and we were still working on their eating habits. Cody sat on the ball-chair every day and read while the other boys learned how to put dishes in the dishwasher. They all learned how to fold towels and sort socks. Now, if we could only teach them to mow the grass! Jim was still trying to do that chore, too.

Slowly, his brain showed signs of deterioration. We had a two-car garage with a dividing column and on more than one occasion, he would catch the driver's side mirror as he was backing out. Too embarrassed to drive the car to an AA meeting with a dangling mirror, I would duct tape it back in place. Sometimes, he would return from work with it dangling again, and I often wondered if he had hit something, or if some annoying students thought it was fun to destroy my handiwork.

Stress was an understatement. I was stressed about that mirror. I wanted the kids to eat right. Building a new house overwhelmed me. I scraped to pay off old debts. And I was watching my husband get sicker every day. I depended on Kathryn to jump-start my day during our morning run. I counted on Bobby to listen to my troubles and help me maintain. And Mike became my tower of strength. When all seemed hopeless, she would enter my world with her bright smiling face, positive attitude, and her overflowing love. She was absolutely beautiful. In the midst of everything, I was truly blessed. I am quite certain it was because we were praying every time we turned around.

Our family made it through the summer and I could not wait for school to start again. The construction of the new house was coming along, and I had formed a good relationship with all the contractors by taking cookies and donuts to them in the mornings. With the boys back in school, I would be able to really pay attention to all the fine details that go into building a house. I was a perfectionist and wanted this new home to be perfect. Do you think I needed AA or what?

In the fall, the Boy Scouts were recruiting new members and I enthusiastically enrolled all the boys in Cub Scouts. I also wanted them to be part of the children's program at church, which consisted of the triplets singing in a choir and Sam playing the chimes; but I had a feeling discipline was a problem with the Three C's. My fears were justified when I began to talk about their participation with one of the choir moms.

Apparently, Jim had wanted them to be active participants, too. The church van picked up the triplets from school, but when they arrived at the church, it was "Katy, bar the door!" The woman, who later became my dear friend, said the triplets were uncontrollable. When the director of the children's choir approached one of the Three C's to quiet his behavior, he proceeded to slap her. They called the triplets' mother, she picked them up, and they didn't come back. Well, this had to change.

The triplets had already met my wooden paddle that an old cowboy made for Sam. You know, the kind that elementary teachers and principals would hang by their door back in the day. Or, maybe you don't. Anyway, Sam was usually pretty well-behaved, but there were a few discipline problems, and that paddle was the way I handled them. It was quick and immediate punishment, and when it was over, it was over. No time-outs or getting grounded. It worked like a charm. I had started bringing this paddle with me to church, and I stayed with the triplets during rehearsal. Several times, I had tried to go without the paddle, but the paddle had been introduced at home, and they were quite familiar with its purpose. I was delighted with their response, so I started taking it to the church services, and figured I could take it to Scouts, too.

That fall, we successfully went to scouts and church, and the boys' behavior was manageable. I involved them in as many activities as possible. I knew it was good for them. I wanted to maintain a normal life as much as possible, and for them to have a good support system. I knew they would need it as their father's illness progressed.

Sixteen

One morning after school had resumed and after I had taken cookies to the contractors, Mike was over having a cup of coffee. We had become very close friends in a very short period. The scout pack had planned a campout and I seriously considered taking the boys.

I proceeded to tell Mike I could borrow a two-room tent and that Sam and I had a smaller, two-man tent still in good shape. We had been camping together before, so I thought this idea might be okay.

After I explained all this to Mike, I could not believe what came out of her mouth. "I'll go with you."

No! She did not know what she was saying. What was she thinking? I tried hard to discourage her. I told her the campsite would be very rough, remote, and the likelihood of running water was just about zero. Mike was determined. She knew I needed help with the boys and all the to-dos that went along with camping, and she insisted on tagging along. God help her!

Jim could not withstand camping. He was exhausted and not feeling well at all, but he could stay by himself. After I shared my thoughts, he told us to go and assured us that all would be fine. He had the numbers of his doctor and friends, and we had cell phones.

It took us days and days to get ready to go. We had found

a camping list online and tried to follow it, but some things seemed ridiculous, so we just crossed them out. We packed the most logical items and checked them off. We had elected to go on Saturday morning instead of Friday night, so we would only spend one night out. We checked the weather channel. Rain was not in the forecast, so we axed the idea of taking ponchos or umbrellas. We were good to go!

We had on our white tennis shoes, cropped jeans, colorful sweaters thrown over our shoulders, and visors on our heads. We may not have been the most experienced campers there, but Mike and I made every effort to be the most fashionable! We laughed at ourselves and made jokes, but we knew deep down that we were going to be very proud of our bravery for taking four little boys camping overnight.

We were not the only ones to arrive on Saturday morning. There was a line to register, and I began to see some adult leaders and people I knew from the Scouts' office. I introduced Mike, and other people I did not know introduced themselves. One of the great things about the Boy Scouts organization is the people. We knew right away that if we needed any help, we could get it. After all, these adults were grown-up Boy Scouts…part of their oath was "to help other people." This was going to be fun.

Keeping four excited, rambunctious boys in line was not an easy task. But we were adamant in enforcing the rule of the buddy system, and I had brought the cowboy paddle. In addition, until we knew more about the camp and what all was going on, I told the boys to stay close to me. They could see ahead of us that other cub scouts were getting surprises as they checked in. I was a little confused, but it appeared each boy was being issued a broomstick. What? Four little boys each loaded with a weapon? I imagined having to break up sword fights. Later, I learned that these sticks would be used in the wood burning session. Why couldn't they just pick up their broomsticks then?

At the registration desk, they gave us a map and told us to drive our vehicle around to our campsite and unload. According to the map, we were on the far side of the canyon, up on a ridge, just below the cap rock, and the hike back would be somewhat of a challenge. When the man at the desk told us we would have to drive our vehicle back around and park in the parking lot after we finished unloading, I said, "We'll see," under my breath.

Mike looked a little concerned. I just winked and cheerfully said, "Okay!"

We found the site and it was beautiful with a magnificent view of the Caprock Escarpment from Camp Post. Mike and I were both glad to be out of the city and among Mother Nature. The boys were so excited that it was hard to keep them focused on the tasks. But we finally got the van unloaded and started to set up camp. We had practiced the night before so we would not look like total idiots trying to set up a tent, and we were finished in about forty minutes. Amazing!

Well, I was almost sure that Mike and I would get to rest, read, and hang our feet in the water, but that was just a dream. Some of the adult leaders came by and told us we needed to help the young scouts with their projects. What? You mean we are going to have to work? My goodness, I thought this was going to be a leisure vacation for us women. Were we expected to help?

The Scouts' projects turned out to be a lot of fun and the sessions were very informative, that is, if you want to know how to shoot arrows and BB guns. You never know when you might need to know some of that stuff, but right then, I couldn't figure out when that possibly might be. The most important thing was that the boys were having a grand time, and Mike and I were feeling useful. It turned out to be a good day.

After lunch, we headed for a leather working session, but soon we were called back to the dining hall. Clouds had built in the northwest and severe thunderstorms were headed our way. When we checked the forecast before we left, there was only a 20% chance of rain, and after living in the Texas Panhandle for thirty-five years, I knew to ignore that kind of percentage. No one paid attention unless there was a 70-90% chance. Go figure!

However, when we looked out from our pavilion, we could see the ominous clouds approaching from the not-so-far-off distance. We headed to the dining hall to watch and wait for the storm to pass. But wait! What about our stuff at the campsite? We had put the rain flaps on the tents (just because everyone else did), but were there other things left out to weather the storm? It was too late to go check. We could not have made the hike and returned to the dining hall without God's fury dumping rain on us.

We were very grateful to be in the dining hall. The sky opened up and the rains came with a fierce wind. The storm ended quickly, but we were afraid our camp was strewn all over the canyon floor. One of the leaders suggested we go check our campsites, and then return to the next session on the afternoon's schedule.

The storm hadn't ended quickly enough to keep from making the campgrounds mighty messy. The red clay soil had gotten muddy and slippery. Also, we are talking canyon here, and you may know what I'm talking about when I say "flash flood." Getting to our campsite was no easy task, as it entailed maneuvering over some crude, unsteady bridges across rushing water and climbing up and down some very slick inclines.

We headed out toward our camp and soon our cute white tennis shoes were not so cute. Heavy, wet, red clay caked onto the soles, and the going got tough. Mike led the way with me and the boys following. We were almost to our site, but we had a very tricky stretch coming up. The trail resembled the back of a camel with steep inclines on both sides. About halfway, between the two humps, Mike slipped. She cried out. I looked up and she was straddling the hump! I rushed to her, grabbed her around the waist, and dug in to get a good footing before I began to hoist her up.

I was trying hard not to laugh because I knew there was a good chance she had stretched those legs just a little too far. Then I heard her. I could not see her face, but I could hear her laughter.

My arms around her waist, I said, "Okay. Ready? Heave!"

We both laughed so hard we could hardly manage. After the third try, Mike got her feet back under her and we regained our composure. It is a good thing she had on that visor, or she would have had a face full of mud. The brim kept her face from hitting rock bottom.

When we reached our camp, we were a mess and you can imagine what the boys looked like. However, our campsite had sustained minimal damage. Our location must have been somewhat protected, because the tents were still standing and everything was in tact. The large tent had some water in the bottom, but our tent was totally dry. Thank goodness I had packed and checked off towels from the list, as these came in very handy mopping up the water. The sun started to come out so we draped them on the trees to dry.

Now it was time to hike back across the canyon for the leather working and wood burning sessions and then supper. I took a deep breath and decided it could not get much worse. How much muddier could we get? I was so proud that our tents were still standing…we were becoming experienced campers very quickly.

At supper, some of the adults and parents talked about packing up and leaving. There was another line of thunderstorms heading our way, but they were not supposed to be severe. Earlier, on the way back to the dining room, Mike had glimpsed a beautiful rainbow and we remembered God's promise. We took it as a sign and decided to stay. We were there, already muddy, and how much worse could it get? What were we thinking? Also, we had decided to leave our van at our campsite until someone told us to move it. No one had, so we knew we could pile in the van for shelter if needed. The boys hooted when we told them our decision to stay.

Remembering the challenges of the trails, we hurriedly finished our supper and headed back to our campsite before it became dark. The scout families were going to have a mock campfire inside that night for the ceremony since the firewood was wet, but Mike and I decided not to attend. If it wasn't for another adult leader who had decided to stay the night too, I doubt we would have had such courage. He also volunteered to watch the boys during the festivities and bring them to our campsite when it was over. What a deal!

That evening, Mike and I sat outside the tent and enjoyed the fresh clean air. The weather was perfect, there were no bugs, and all seemed right with God. We finally got the relaxing quiet time we had craved, and we were truly "hanging our feet in the water." It was a very special time for two best friends and one that neither one of us will ever forget.

The boys returned about 10:00 and I gave them all orders to use the bathroom and do everything they wanted to do *before* they got into their tent. The ground was still very muddy, and I wanted to prevent the boys from creating mud floors in their tents. Wet, dirty clothes and shoes remained outside; cozy, warm bedrolls inside called for some very tired little boys.

Mike and I followed suit. We made our way to the latrine, which was little more than a hole in the ground surrounded by wooden walls. There were no "men" or "women" facilities; we all used the same one. Inside, the latrine was dark, damp, stinky, and full of spider webs. We would not be bringing a magazine!

Armed with flashlights, we escorted each other and took our turns. With that little chore behind us, we headed back to our tent. We had a nice queen-size air mattress, and I silently prayed it would still have air in the morning. Surely, God would be good to us one more time. We settled in and noted the time: 10:30 p.m. and all was well.

At exactly 10:31 p.m., it began to rain. It poured and poured and poured. Not a storm, just a steady gentle rain. ZZZzzzzz. The boys must have been sound asleep because I did not hear a peep from their tent.

Mike and I talked and laughed about all the events of the day, and how nice it was to have an air mattress and a dry tent. We could see the water dripping down the sides of our tent, and we wondered how we would ever top this experience.

Around 2:00 a.m. the rain stopped. Yea! Neither of us

wanted to say a word, but the rain had given us both the urge to go to the bathroom. We had not gotten much sleep and I knew if I did not get up and go to the bathroom, I would not sleep for the rest of the night.

Mike stirred and I said, "I need to go to the bathroom."

She laughed. "So do I!"

We ooched our way to the opening of our tent and stuck our legs out to put on our shoes. We found our flashlights and headed that way. Rounding the corner, we both stopped dead in our tracks. There was a light in the latrine! Who could it be? We both stood there, not knowing what to do or say. It never occurred to us there would be a line at 2:00 a.m. My urge to relieve my bladder was getting the best of me.

Mike whispered, "Is someone in there?"

"I don't know," I whispered back, "but there's only one way to find out." In a somewhat lame, shaky voice, I said, "Hello?"

A man's voice said hello back, and instantly we knew it was Pat, the other adult leader who had also decided to stay. Mike and I broke out laughing. I could not stand it. I left her standing there and I made a beeline for the bushes.

Moments later, we were snuggled back into our sleeping bags, and the air mattress held up beautifully. Then, completely exhausted, we slept.

We did not stir until the boys' chatter woke us the next morning. What I overheard was not exactly what I wanted to hear.

The boys complained they were soaking wet. They must have been so tired that they didn't notice the cold and the dampness, but they sure felt it this morning. We weren't sure, but we thought maybe the rain flaps on their tent weren't as efficient as they should have been. We had used our only tarp under their tent, and luckily, our air mattress had kept us atop the swimming pool in our tent. Of course, all of our towels still hung in the trees, wetter than ever and totally useless.

I started barking orders. All I wanted to do was throw everything in the back of the van, go eat a hot breakfast, and head home. I'd had all the fun I could stand. We were still trying to keep our sense of humor, but when four little boys are whining and their discomfort is more than noticeable, it's time to make a change. When Pat and his son had their gear all loaded up, they came and lent us a hand. In just minutes, we had broken down camp and packed everything up. I should not say packed, because we just crammed everything in, mud and all!

Pat explained how to navigate the road back around to the front of the Boy Scout camp, and I vaguely remembered him describing a low, unpaved area; when it rained, water rushed over that stretch of road. The surrounding landscape looked like marshland. Gently, he tried to say there was a very good possibility I would get stuck. Oh, brother! What next? He assured me I would be okay if I just kept a steady push on the accelerator to get through. What else could we do but try?

He let us go first and when I reached that mud pit in the road, I pushed on the accelerator with all my might! I know I was pushing down a little too hard, but since I had been raised on a farm, I had watched my dad barrel his way through worse mud puddles, amazed that he did not get stuck. I knew we had to push the pedal to the metal; to slow down would be the death of us. Well, not death exactly, but someone would have to be called to tow us out.

Out of the corner of my eye, I saw Mike praying very hard.

"Look out! We're coming through!" I yelled.

Mud and water flew everywhere. Mike's eyes grew wide and her white knuckles clenched the dash. My adrenaline rushed sky high. It was either make it or break it, right then and there.

At last, the van reached the end of the flooded road, and

I released my breath as the tires trundled over stable ground. We made it! There were shouts of joy from everyone. I slowed down as we made the curve that headed to the dining hall. There wasn't much left in the way of challenges now; all we had to do was feed these little boys and head home. We parked as close to the entrance as possible, and as we all piled out of the van it began to rain again.

As we entered the dining room, people looked at us with surprise. Then, they began to applaud. Very few people had stayed the night, and apparently, word had gotten around about us. We got congratulations, high fives, and pats on the back. The adults were amazed we had stayed, and a few told us how proud they were of us.

There was no explaining the feelings both Mike and I had at that moment. We were elated. We felt like superwomen. We had taken four little boys camping and we knew in our hearts that the triplets would probably never get another chance. We definitely made some fine memories that weekend.

Seventeen

Jim finished taking radiation treatments about the same time school started for the fall semester that year. We were dreading chemo treatment like the plague because we knew it made some people deathly ill. We also realized that some people opted not to take chemo, and chose to let the cancer run its course to avoid being sick. Of course, that was out of the question in our case, because we knew there was a miracle in store for us. We refused to believe that the tumor would win.

The kids had gone back to school. Mike and I maintained a good friendship and met for coffee once a week with our new friends from church. In addition, I had joined a cancer support group and insisted on Jim and I attending once a week in the evenings. I still went to AA most of the time, and Jim usually attended those meetings with me. I reached out to every resource I could muster because I wanted to feel okay. I was past *fine*. Lesson learned. There is no way to feel *fine* when someone you love is terminally ill.

When we arrived at the cancer group as newcomers, as in most group meetings, there was the routine of introductions and going around the circle, taking turns sharing personal stories. When my turn came, I quickly told about how Jim and I met, about our family and the triplets, and how Jim had been diagnosed with an inoperable brain tumor. After the meeting, one of the women came over, gave me a hug, and held on for the longest time. I wondered why, but she knew. She knew without a doubt that Jim would eventually die.

Jim always wanted to go to new places to experience new things. There was nothing better than discovering something new and sharing it with the one you love. That fall, we attended a musical production at Tech. We knew some of the students, because they were associate members of our church. During the production, one of the students approached us and asked if she could dedicate a song to Jim. Once again, I wondered why, but now I know. She, too, knew something we refused to believe.

There was such goodness in all the wonderful people who knew Jim. Soon after he was diagnosed, one of the secretaries from his office called to say how distressed they were with the news. She said they wanted us to know how concerned they were and how the news had taken all the employees by storm. They were in shock and wanted us to know they were very upset. Why were they taking this so hard? Because they knew he would die. Jim and I were in denial and we held onto the belief that he would be cured. We had our faith. Was it faith? Was it believing only what we wanted to believe? Or just plain ignorance?

We did not care. We showed everyone on the outside looking in that we were brave, immortal, and that we had everything under control. We were *fine*. Others may have seen us as invincible, but we were crumbling on the inside. Jim drank more and I felt smothered. Our life had been reduced to taking him for treatments and taking care of the boys.

* * *

One weekend, one of the boys mentioned riding their bikes to school. How exciting! I had promoted to them the idea of walking home in the afternoons, why couldn't they get themselves to school as well? This would be great! I would not have to take them to school unless it was raining or snowing. I was fooling myself, of course. I had an uncanny way of complicating our lives when AA was forever preaching to "KISS... Keep It Simple Stupid."

Like an idiot, I did not think to check the tires on the bikes on Sunday night to see if they were aired up. Since we lived only a block and a half from school, I sent the boys on their way about thirty minutes before the tardy bell. I was not thinking! I failed to think about the tires or about Cody and his weak muscles. Since he was struggling at school, his backpack was always loaded down with extra work, and it was heavy. This was a disaster ready to happen.

I patiently waited for the boys to get home and started getting nervous when they did not show up at the scheduled time. Finally, Sam arrived and explained the incident.

Back when we lived in Colorado City, Sam and I had ridden bikes, and after dealing with many flats, I had installed airless inner tubes in our tires. However, while they were riding home that afternoon, the tires on the triplets' bikes all went flat. Sam explained how hard it was for Cody to get to school and how he was exhausted and in tears when he finally entered his classroom. As Sam finished the story, Cooper and Caleb arrived out of breath and with their tongues hanging out.

"Where's Cody?" I asked, feeling concerned.

"He's still trying to get home," his brothers said.

I instructed the boys to sit at the table and start on homework, then I dashed out the door to rescue Cody. My heart was racing. I knew I had made a bad mistake. I found him close to the school, in tears. I jumped out from the van and ran over to him. I took Cody in my arms. My heart melted. I have never felt such compassion for another child. He was crying, and I kept saying, "I'm am so sorry, Cody. Please, please forgive me."

It was hard to understand what he was saying, but I was pretty sure he was cursing me and swearing off bicycles for good. I took him home to join the others doing homework. Something changed that day. God had intervened. From then on, I was just a tad gentler when it came to Cody. He had stolen my heart.

* * *

The next morning, after court and before breakfast, I aired up all the tires. They were good to go. *Let's try this again!* This time, I walked along with Cody. I made sure he got to school on time and encouraged him to keep trying. I wanted him to feel good about himself. I also knew the exercise would help build his thigh muscles.

We did it! Everyone got to school on time and Cody was happy. Although tired from riding his bike, he would gain strength, and every day that he made it to school on time would build his confidence. I was such a fool!

I did not think that the tires might go flat again during the day. Sam arrived on time, but Cooper and Caleb arrived a little later.

"Where is Cody?" I asked.

"Guess!" his brothers said.

"Get out your homework and get to work," I ordered.

I had made another bad mistake. This time, I could not convince Cody to try riding his bike to school again. I could not blame him. I had thrown him in the fire twice, and he was smart enough not to fall for it again. I replaced all the inner tubes and we were good to go. As the other boys rode their bikes, I drove Cody to school. However, when we got there, I had to make sure I understood what he was saying. He wanted me to bring his bike to school so he could ride it home with the other boys. Yes! I had not given Cody enough credit. At that moment, I felt like he might have what it takes to get by in this world, even with the odds against him. I was so proud! I grew to love him more every day.

That afternoon, I arrived at school with the bike. We then proceeded to head home, nice and slow. Cooper rode his bike first, then Sam, then Caleb followed, and finally Cody pedaled his bike as I drove alongside him in my van. Everything seemed right. The day was beautiful, the tires had air in them, Cody was trying again, and I was witnessing his triumph!

An SUV drove in front of the van, about even with Caleb, and the traffic moved along leisurely. I could see Cooper way ahead, followed by Sam. Then suddenly, I could not believe my eyes! Caleb had turned around to say something to Cody and veered directly into the SUV's front tire! We were moving slowly, but not slow enough. The impact threw Caleb off his bike. Clearly hurt, he lay on the ground, crying.

I jumped out of the van and ran to Caleb. The woman driving the SUV sat behind the wheel, in shock. I could not believe this was happening. I shouted at Sam. Cooper was too far ahead to hear, but Cody was right there. We all witnessed what every parent dreads.

Caleb wailed and grabbed his scraped knee. His elbow was bleeding, but other than that, he seemed fine.

I shouted orders for Sam to get Caleb's bicycle in the van and for Cody to ride on home. I intended to pick up Caleb and take him home, but it was too late. People had already gathered, and some strange man was not going to let me pick up Caleb.

The man claimed to be an EMT and tried to explain that a car had just hit my child.

No, that did not happen. Did you see it? Did you see what happened? A car did not hit Caleb. Caleb hit the SUV!

Besides, we could not call an ambulance. What would Jim think? What would everyone think? Here I was supposed to be superwoman, and now I appeared to be an incompetent stepmother. How could I let this happen? How on earth was I going to explain this to anyone? The crowd around me was spinning. All I wanted was to take Caleb home, put a bandage on his wounds, fix the bike, and go on living without a big production. Couldn't this man understand?

Mr. EMT was adamant. He almost got nasty when I told him I was going to take Caleb home. I told Sam to go home and call Jim at work. Cooper had already left. Cody stayed with us as we waited for the ambulance, for Jim, and for the television cameras. What? You guessed it. The whole thing would be televised that night on the local news. My incredible stupidity was going to be shown to the whole world. I was really hating life about now.

Jim arrived shortly after the ambulance, and some of the parents of the neighborhood offered to see after the boys, while Jim and I stayed at the hospital with Caleb. The news cameraman turned out to be a member of our church and notified our pastor, Kathryn. We were not in the emergency room long before she arrived and said prayers with us. Luckily, Caleb had no broken bones, just severe cuts and bruises. We were able to take him home that evening, but life did not go on as usual for quite a few more days.

* * *

The phone rang constantly. Caleb stayed home from school for a couple of days and everyone was concerned. Teachers, friends, relatives, church members, co-workers, and acquaintances called to ask about his condition. I often wondered if that was the purpose, or if they just wanted to know if I was close to losing my mind. I was and I knew it. I called Dr. Kim and got a referral to a psychiatrist. When Caleb went back to school, I went to see the shrink.

After explaining the situation from start to present, she told me I needed to send the triplets to their mother.

"No!" I argued. "I can't do it!"

In the first place, sending the boys away would devastate Sam, and it would appear that we were giving up. Besides, I wanted the triplets to stay with their dad as long as possible. I knew their presence was good for Jim. If they were gone, he would give up and his health would deteriorate quickly. His sons were living with us for a purpose, and I did not care if I died in the process; we were going to stay together as a family as long as possible.

My psychiatrist asked, "So, do you want me to give you something to help deal with what you refuse to give up?"

Yes, please! Give me drugs. Give me something to help me maintain. I felt like I was treading water in an ocean and could not see land in any direction.

"Okay," she said, as she wrote out a prescription. "I call it the 'don't sweat the small stuff' pill." She said I would not care if the boys' socks were blue. I wouldn't care if they wore socks at all!

Wonderful! Give them here.

I took a small pill once a day and it was magical. It was just another Godsend during those times, or maybe I should say my therapist was a Godsend. Anyway, I was on meds and able to maintain. I did not *sweat the small stuff* anymore. It was a good thing because I had plenty of *big stuff* to sweat over.

Eighteen

On top of all I was dealing with, right before Christmas, I got bit by a brown recluse spider. Jim had a small storage building in the back yard, and we kept our Christmas tree hanging on the back wall. Once again, I was not thinking. Even though the building stayed damp from the sprinkler system, and even though it was dark inside most of the time, I did not think about spiders. And the only thing I knew about recluse spiders was from looking at pictures in magazines of peoples' skin rotting off from the poison.

It was tradition for my family to put the tree up over the Thanksgiving holidays. Usually, Derek brought the tree in because it was heavy and awkward. This year, he was spending Thanksgiving with his grandparents and he was not around. I reached behind the tree to lift it off the hooks and never felt that little devil bite me. It started as a small blister and I did not think much of it until I showed my wound to Mike at church on Sunday.

"Oh, my gosh!" she exclaimed. "Lynette, you've been bitten by a brown recluse spider!"

"Oh, *pshaw*. That's nonsense." I waved it off like it was no big deal, but my hand was really hurting.

Nonetheless, Mike would not let the matter go. A recluse had bitten her on the toe years ago, so she knew how serious its bite could be. That Sunday afternoon, she insisted we go to a walk-in clinic.

The doctor cleaned the wound, I got a shot of a high-powered antibiotic, then she sent us on our way. She said to come back first thing in the morning. If the wound was not any better, she was going to recommend a hand specialist. The sore spot was on the middle finger of my right hand, and you guessed it, I am right-handed.

Now, what else could go wrong? You think I still had faith that God was going to take care of us? Can you imagine what it would be like to have a sick husband, four kids, and a right hand that did not work, and right before Christmas? It was near impossible, and I can tell you that from experience.

The hand specialist was the same doctor that treated Jim's broken tendon from the basketball injury. I am not so sure she was glad to see me. I had been a little perturbed when she couldn't fix Jim's middle finger. *Now, let's see you fix mine, and I need it done before Christmas.* There was some friction between us, to say the least.

However, any conflict we had did not last. As she was examining my rotting finger, I began to tell her about our misfortune. I had been *fine* up to that point. The tears came and I confided in her not as a patient, but as a client who needed intensive inpatient treatment. I bared my soul, explaining that no matter how hard I tried to keep things right, time after time something always went wrong. I felt ready to give up.

The hand specialist grafted my finger that same afternoon, and during one of the follow-up appointments, she advised me to call Hospice. *Wait! Hospice is just for people who are dying!* She knew, but I refused to believe. She gently said it was not just for people who were at that point, but they had counseling for the family members, for grieving, and for all stages of any terminal illness. I was at my wits' end. The little "don't sweat the small stuff" pill was still working, but I needed more.

I decided to call Hospice.

Jim was hurt. "What? You called Hospice?"

"Yes." I needed help dealing with all of this, and I needed help dealing with his drinking. He could stay home or he could come with me. It was his choice. Of course, he came because he did not want me talking about him in his absence. It occurred to me that he was going to AA for that purpose, too. But Hospice? You guessed it. Neither of us said anything because we had promised each other not to talk about *death*. Besides, we were both still in denial.

I added another weekly appointment to our already overscheduled calendar. It was insane. I kept trying to keep it together when, in fact, I was cluttering up our lives. I had coffee with the Lazy Mothers group on Tuesday mornings. I went with the boys to Scouts on Monday nights and the whole family attended church on Wednesday evenings. Tuesday and Thursday evenings were AA and cancer support group meetings. I saw my psychiatrist every Monday, and Jim and I had a standing appointment on Thursday mornings at Hospice. We visited the chemo doctor every three weeks and the neurosurgeon once a month. We held a prayer meeting every morning with Kathryn, and Cody went to therapy on Tuesday after school. I was so busy trying to stay sane, I didn't have time to go crazy. In addition to all this craziness, Jim was still holding court at 5:00 in the mornings, four days a week.

Who said, "Keep it simple, stupid"? I was doing all the wrong things for our family, but I did not see any other way to survive. Everything we were involved in seemed like an essential need for survival. I was running myself ragged, dragging Jim and the children along, and did not even realize it. Why didn't someone say something? In the meantime, we were building a new house. *Arghhhh!*

Keep it simple? Are they crazy? I am a recovered alcoholic! Nothing is simple.

Adding to my roller-coaster madness, the boys wanted a new pet. What is it with kids and pets? Why do they think animals are so terrific? They wanted an iguana.

"No."

"How about a rabbit?"

"No."

"A snake?"

"Absolutely not."

"A gerbil? A parakeet? A puppy?"

"No, no, and no."

We already had an outside dog and I just could not take care of one more living thing. However, when the boys begged and pleaded for a cat, I finally succumbed. "Okay, we'll get a cat." Once again I was not thinking.

Jim had told me before that he was allergic to cats, but I figured if we were going to get a new pet, a cat would be the easiest to take care of. When I asked him about it, he confessed he only professed to be allergic to cats because he did not want to own one. Well, this might be the ticket. I could teach the boys some responsibility and a cat would not be that much trouble. All I had to do was set out food and water and make sure the litter box was clean. If we could find one that was litter-box trained and could stand being tormented by four boys, we would be in luck. I called the humane society.

Sure enough, the lady said we could come over and have our pick. There were cats everywhere! Hanging off the already shredded drapes in the living room. Involved in catfights in the kitchen. This was a haven for homeless cats. The poor cat lady could not bear the thought of lessening her burden. She scurried around and picked the "perfect" cat for us.

She said, "This one is a little spitfire. He can take care of himself and he can handle the boys." He was a beautiful white and black kitten with green eyes.

Immediately, Cooper said, "We can name it Spitfire!" as he pried the kitten out of her hands. Thus, Spitfire joined the Albright household.

*　*　*

Spitfire could not have come at a better time. That weekend, Jim had tapered off the steroids the doctor had given him for inflammation, and his brain began to swell. We called them "episodes" for lack of a better term, and he had the first one on Saturday morning.

He woke up unable to speak or stand. I was beside myself, absolutely terrified that this was the end. I called the doctor's answering service, and when he called back, I quickly explained what was happening. He assured me Jim's condition was caused by inflammation, and if I would give him double doses of the steroids, it would help and he would return to normal. Normal. I did not even know what *normal* meant anymore.

I gave Jim the steroids, but all day he was unable to take care of himself. He could not feed himself, hold a glass, speak, walk, or communicate. I prayed harder that day than I had ever prayed before. With God's help, we made it through that episode, but not without trials and tribulations. I had never cared for an invalid in my life, and I did not have a clue what I was doing. Fortunately, the boys had Spitfire to keep them entertained and did not even notice the situation with their dad. It was truly amazing how things worked out, and how God directed us to do things that seemed entirely pointless at the time. Spitfire saved us that weekend. I have no doubts. You see? Just another Godsend.

The weekend seemed endless and by Sunday night I was exhausted. Finally, Jim began to return to his old self, but I was in tears when I called his friend, Terry, that evening. I was emotionally distraught as I explained what had happened and told him he needed to hurry and finish that house, because I feared Jim wouldn't last much longer.

Jim was okay by Monday morning and able to go to work. By this time, I was driving him to work after taking the boys to school. Our bicycling days were over. I discovered that being a control freak often had its advantages. The more I could control, the less mishaps and disasters occurred. Just another one of those things AA tried to teach but did not quite sink in, and for this particular time, that was a good thing.

Throughout his illness, we encountered many of those brain-swelling episodes, and each time Jim recovered, he didn't return to where he was before. We lessened the dose of steroids, because we were told how damaging they were if a person stayed on them for very long, but what was the worse of two evils? When he did not take steroids, we had episodes, and when he took them, we did not have episodes. But we also had the danger of being exposed to too many steroids for too long a period. We could not win for losing.

* * *

I got a fresh idea for Christmas that year. Traditionally, Jim and the boys' mom had bought gifts for all the boys to share, and their way of opening presents was a free for all. But now that they were living with me and Jim, I decided to start our own tradition. Since I had gotten to know Cooper, Caleb, and Cody on a personal level, I decided to shop for them individually. From Santa, they would have personalized gifts picked especially for them. A pretty clever idea, right?

Boy, did I ever get a shot in the arm! The boys woke up on Christmas morning excited to see what Santa had brought. They ran into the living room and started grabbing presents.

"Wait!" I halted them with my shout. "Cody, that is not yours. It's Caleb's."

"What?"

"Cooper, that was not in your stocking."

"I wanted that!"

"This is mine!"

"No, it's not!"

"This isn't fair!"

Tears started flowing as the boys got angry and frustrated. Sam tried to referee and justify certain gifts for certain boys, but it wasn't working. The more we tried to explain, the worse it got. I pulled Sam away and told him to get dressed. I threw on a pair of jeans and we headed out the door.

Another lesson learned. Control issues are NOT okay all the time. If it isn't broke, don't fix it. The triplets had been doing Christmas a certain way for five years, and I came in and tried to change it. What had I done? I had screwed up the whole holiday experience for everyone. Leaving Jim to deal with the boys, I ran off with Sam in tow—on Christmas morning! What were we going to do? Nothing was open, it was freezing cold, and we had no place to go. What was I thinking?

Not much time passed before I realized we needed to go home. After all, Derek, Jon, and Josh were all coming over for Christmas dinner and I had to get it together before they arrived. A few weeks before, they had magically appeared at a family portrait setting, and I now felt compelled to show my gratitude. Not to mention, I had made a big mistake walking out on Jim and his sons, and I needed to see if I could put the pieces back together. I expected to walk into pure bedlam, but what I saw shocked me into a state of total disbelief.

Cooper, Caleb, and Cody were all huddled in the living room, playing quietly together, and all getting along! This must have been God's work. I could not imagine any other power intervening and working miracles. The triplets were actually happy, and I had nothing to do with it. Apparently, with their dad's help, they had managed to work things out. I imagined Jim calmly reminding them to share and persuading them all to believe in the "what's mine is yours" theory.

Sam and I joined the party. Once again, I was thanking God for the small blessings He was forever bestowing upon me.

I tried to keep things simple on Christmas Day and almost succeeded. My right hand still wasn't working, and to serve dinner to nine people was almost overwhelming. However, the older boys arrived and helped as much as I would let them. Dinner turned out great, the fellowship was even better, and we created another positive family memory. God was indeed great, and He guided us through yet another disaster. How did I deserve such grace? God was thinking for me.

Lynette,

I could have told you long ago,
When I first took your kiss.
That some day love would laugh at us
And life would be like this.
I knew that time would change the world.
And we would never be.
Contented in each others arms.
For all eternity.
But when I saw you smile at me,
I felt that you would cry.
If ever I should turn to you,
And say a last good-by.
And so I never spoke a word.
Or ever let you know.
That we would be as changeble,
As are the winds that blow.
But I was certain in my heart.
That there would come a day.
When dreams would end and you and,
Would have to go away.

Love.
Jim

Nineteen

Few of us really knows how we would act or how we would think or feel if we discovered we were terminally ill. Even though Jim refused to let anyone know if he thought he might die, he must have known on the inside. I am not sure if it was the tumor taking over his brain or just the terrible knowledge that his future had been trashed. Sometimes, I believe he knew and wanted to talk about it, but maybe he was trying to save face, or save me. I wish I knew all the answers.

But imagine! Here he was. He had found the love of his life (and I never once doubted he loved me totally) and a good stepmom for his children. His church and community admired him; he was a well-respected lawyer; and he was a director of a legal services department at a major university, yet his future was destroyed. He would not get to grow old, see his young triplets grow up, or experience grandchildren. How could he not be at least a little angry?

Jim was losing his sight and losing his ability to be a contributing part of the family. As the days wore on, he interacted less with us, and subsided more and more into his easy chair, his bourbon, and his books on tape. He still showed up for work at the office, but his presence there was useless. I guess we were all trying to save his dignity. His co-workers handled the situation wonderfully. They let him keep his nice, cushy office. He kept the door closed, set up headphones to a stereo, and listened to my pick of audio tapes from the library. He never, ever complained.

His memory faded fast. He could not remember where the bathroom was located, so when he needed to find it, his secretary had to show him the way. Someone else down the hall would wait for him to come out to lead him back to his chair. Can you imagine the frustration and fear this man faced every day? On the other hand, did he even realize what was happening? I commended him for just getting out of bed in the morning. I would have been tempted to just crawl under the covers and die.

You see! I cannot tell you how many times I said, "I would handle this so differently! I would be the life of the party, and if there was not a party around, I would find one. I would want to experience life to the fullest, do things, go places, and see everything I could." But then again, would I have been able, or would I have really wanted to do everything I could, if there was this huge mass of tissue invading my brain?

I wish I could measure how much energy I spent trying to draw my husband out of his shell and stay with the human race. I tried and tried to get him to talk and communicate his innermost thoughts, but it was no use. I found him crying from time to time, and I suggested he talk to someone other than me. He agreed and I called Kathryn or Bobby, but by the time they got there, Jim had forgotten why they'd come to visit, what he wanted to say, or if he wanted to say anything at all. To him, they were just paying a courtesy call.

I stayed frustrated and angry about 90% of the time. Many times I called my counselor, Robert, at Hospice to discuss Jim's drinking and his desire to isolate himself. I told my counselor how I just wanted Jim to act alive until he was, in fact, dead. Sometimes, I got so mad at his ability to escape; I wanted to pour the bourbon straight down the sink! You see, I was beginning to believe he would not live, so I wanted to make the most of what time we had left together. But Jim was not cooperating. I was totally exasperated.

The quantity of bourbon in his drinks was always a battle between us. He made them so strong. He drank excessively, endangering his well-being. He had even fallen and caved in the bathroom wall and broken a wooden shutter in the bedroom. One day, during our session at Hospice, I mentioned this "little" problem.

Robert and I agreed that it would be too harsh to make Jim quit drinking altogether, so we were trying to find a solution. Robert's intern was in the room and she suggested that I set out little plastic containers with measured shots in each one for Jim's quota for the night. All I needed was one more daily chore to add to the mix! I could only imagine the resentment I would develop over those five or six little containers.

Then, one night at AA I remembered the little slogan "Be and let be." Those words saved my sanity. I never got any peace until I realized there was nothing I could do about the situation. To keep trying to control Jim, control the way he thought and the progress of his illness was a waste of time and precious energy. I had to "Let go and let God," one of the hardest lessons this alcoholic had to learn. It was still all about giving up my need to control.

However, I was still boss in this household, and I could control Jim's drinking to some extent. I agreed to fill a pint bottle each day and when he finished it, no more for the rest of the evening. Everyone at Hospice agreed that was a workable solution. It worked great until Jim started accusing me of filling it up only halfway or not at all. I gave up. I started mixing his drinks stiffer and not measuring. All I could do was try to keep him from hurting himself or us. As they say, "Choose your battles wisely." I did not want to fight this one, and I felt it was best for him to win.

* * *

Even though overseeing construction of the new house had been a major pain, it turned out to be a blessing for all of us. Eventually, thanks to Terry and his crew, we finished building our dream house. The move was total chaos, and I did not think I would ever get through the sea of boxes. However, Mike helped see us through the whole mess. She even unpacked the kitchen one morning while I went with Jim to the doctor's office. Mike was amazing and after all her help the house looked awesome!

Each of the boys had their own room and a place they could go for "time out" (yes, did not need the paddle anymore), solace, or privacy. Even though all the boys were at each other's throats most of the time, there was no problem in deciding who got what room. Previously, I had seen the handwriting on the wall, so I had laid out the plans, showed them the bedrooms, and let them pencil in the room they wanted. I watched in fear as they studied and conversed, and I was stunned when they had picked their room without drawing any blood.

Again, God worked miracles.

Jim's eyes even twinkled when we moved in and he realized we did not have to go back to the other house. He looked all around and grinned from ear to ear. He said, "I feel like we are in a luxury hotel, and it is home!"

Yes, indeed, it was home and yet another Godsend. I have no doubts that I would have lost all my sanity if we had stayed in the little house under the growing challenges of everyday life. I had even suggested to Terry to make the master bedroom and bath handicapped ready. He was the one who thought of the heightened toilet. You, go, Terry!

Never think you don't need two dishwashers. Another blessing. I would never be without clean dishes again! We had two microwaves; one strictly for the boys. We bought a new refrigerator, so the old one was set up in the garage for overflow. Best of all, the master bedroom was right by the kitchen and my coffee pot within arm's reach! The plans were fit to order. I could be in the kitchen working while keeping an eye on Jim in the bedroom. As we all settled in, we thought we had found Heaven on earth.

The neighborhood was great, too. Another set of triplets lived just down the street, and a family of six kids a block away. Our new house was located on a cul-de-sac and I felt my family was safe. We set up our basement as a game room, and when the kids were home and not outside, I barely knew they were there. Everything seemed perfect, except for the fact that my husband was dying.

Cody was doing well in school and it looked like he might pass the second grade. You go, Cody! I will never forget what happened the day Cody and I were at the kitchen table after I had visited with one of his teachers at school. He and I were still having our reading and homework sessions, but it was still very unpleasant. Cody never wanted to sit; he wanted to be playing with his brothers or the neighborhood kids. I understood, but I knew how important an education was, and I was not going to let him fall through the cracks. You see, I still had a control issue.

When we finished, I told Cody I had talked to his teacher, and she told me how very proud they were of him. He seemed happier, more content, his self-esteem had shot way up, and he could look people in the eye now as he spoke. His grades were good, his writing skills excellent, and his improvement outstanding. I shared all this with him as he looked me in the eye and blinked.

He said, "Really, Mom?"

I smiled. "Really, Cody. You did it. You really did it. I knew you could."

All of a sudden, he hopped up out of his chair and threw his arms around me, and buried his head in my neck. "Thanks, Mom. I love you."

I held him until he broke away. He skipped off and my jaw hit the floor. You see, he had not been able to skip before now. The physical therapist had tried to teach him, but with no luck. We had all tried to teach him, but he just couldn't get it. Here he was, skipping off to join his brothers. I sat at the kitchen table and cried, embracing the moment.

Just days before, I had the notion to teach Cody to tie his shoes. I kid you not; we sat on the kitchen floor for an hour and a half, learning to tie a bow. It became another battle for control. He was not going to learn, but oh, yes, he was! Once again, I told him, "You might as well just give it up and learn, Cody. We are not going to get up from this spot until you have successfully mastered tying your shoes."

UGH! We were both exhausted and I was quite sure he hated me. However, he learned how to tie his shoes and was noticeably happy about that.

* * *

The boys still struggled with food issues, but since they were eating healthy, the regularity of sicknesses went way down. Cody was still guilty of getting a mouthful of something he did not like, then excusing himself to the bathroom. We wised up. When we figured it out, we made him go to the bathroom before we sat down, and we made him show us his empty mouth if he claimed he needed to go. Caleb had quit throwing up on his plate, and Cooper, well, Cooper, was a different story. He would eat anything and have second or third helpings. No problem there. I heehawed that year when they all came home with Thanksgiving projects of what they were thankful for, and three out of four boys said, "Mom's cooking!" Yeah, right. Pinch me, I'm dreaming.

We kept on living, but things got harder and harder. Even though Jim was only 55, he seemed much older. We were still going to work, to church, doctors' appointments, cancer support group meetings, AA, and he still worked as magistrate for the city. Sometimes, his lawyer friends would pick him up from the office to go to lunch, but when Jim lost his way back to the table from the buffet, they decided they would bring lunch to Jim. It was nice for him to have such loyal friends.

I took him everywhere, escorting him in, and I did most of the work for him at the detention center at 5:00 in the mornings. We really needed the money to cover the new house payment, and I did not see how we could manage if he lost either the job at Tech or the magistrate position with the city. I started making a few phone calls to see *What if...?*

First, I called Social Security. I did not expect much help, but when I told her our situation, the woman suggested we fill out disability forms and come in for an interview immediately. I made an appointment, we signed up, and it was not long before we started receiving payments. Next, I called Texas Tech University and talked to the head of the personnel department.

Wow! Jim had so much sick time built up; he could stay sick for a year and would still be able to draw a full salary. We could draw disability payments at the same time because he was actually unable to work. This was great news. With the child support from their mom, we could manage. Yes! Goodness, we had gotten out from under a $10,000 credit card bill, so I knew we could do this. I was a little reluctant to speak to

Jim about quitting work, but it was time. Staying at the office was taking its toll on him, and I was worn out from trying to live a lie. Jim was dying, and even if he did not know it, I did.

I called city hall and talked to the judge. He was very compassionate but I could hear relief in his voice. I'm sure he had gotten wind that I was holding court on the mornings we were scheduled, and all I had was a business degree. He said he was very sorry for Jim's illness and wanted to help if he could, but I could tell he was very relieved we would not be setting foot in his courtroom again. I was relieved too, ready to stop pretending to be something I was not.

As I explained to Jim all that I had discovered, the tension left his face. I thought he might have trouble understanding, but he comprehended everything I told him about vacation time, sick leave, disability, and social security. It was as though a big burden lifted off his shoulders. He was tired of going to work, but more than that, he knew what a burden it was on me to continue doing everything for him. He was indeed an angel—my angel—and I loved him more at that moment than I had ever loved him before. There is such sweet release when one surrenders to the inevitable. Jim knew there was no returning to work and he wanted to lessen my load.

In some ways, it had been easier to take Jim to work in the mornings and pick him up in the afternoons. Sure, it was a bit of a hassle, but there was a certain comfort when he was away. You see, I did not have to face our calamity when he was out of the house. While home alone, I could forget I had four children in my charge and was caretaker of a terminally ill patient. On the other hand, with Jim at home full time, there was no escaping reality. It was in my face every day, 24/7.

When their dad started staying home from work, the boys figured out he was really sick. He sat in his chair all day, drank bourbon, and listened to books. Cooper, Caleb, and Cody were angels, too. It was so sweet to watch them care for their dad. They would lead him around and find his glasses (not that he could see much anymore). The triplets would help him fill his plate at the table, and when the stereo's tape player stopped, they would switch tapes and restart them. They could not do enough for their dad, and it was charming to observe the role reversals. In some ways, I wanted time to stop. This was manageable. In an eerie sort of way, this household almost seemed normal.

*   *   *

We really did not know how much time Jim and I had left together, but Mike had a good idea. She had watched her husband die, and she could see how Jim's body and mind were deteriorating. She suggested I have a conversation with the triplets' mother and discuss what to do in a worst-case scenario. Their mother had not seen Jim in some time, but she also knew the end was near. We talked about the transition of moving the boys from our house to hers. It was something we were all dreading, but we knew this transition was inevitable. She told me the boys were hers and that she would raise them. The day the boys moved out was going to be a sad day indeed.

I cannot say enough about Mike. She had thought about going to see her kids over the Thanksgiving holidays, but she elected to stay here and help me have the best Thanksgiving celebration ever! This was our year to have the triplets for the holiday. Josh had moved away, but Jon was going to be here. It was always tradition for Derek to spend Thanksgiving with us instead of his father's parents. Mike started planning the dinner, and as I listened, I was amazed.

She came over bright and early Thanksgiving Day loaded with goodies. She brought and prepared almost everything but the turkey. I had insisted on cooking the holiday bird and the bread. Mike brought crafts for the boys to keep them busy until dinner. Their assignment was to make the placemats and place cards with craft paper, holiday stickers and leaves to glue on for decorations. Mike even brought fresh flowers and a small pumpkin and made a magnificent centerpiece for the table.

She was so efficient and so beautiful; how she managed to bring warmth and glow to our holiday get-together was unbelievable. The day and meal turned out perfect. I had truly been blessed when God put Mike in my life. I could have sworn I saw a halo over her head from time to time; she was the epitome of grace and goodness. I was so grateful to have all the boys with us, to have Jim sitting at the head of the table, and to enjoy this Thanksgiving…the one I knew would be our last as a family.

* * *

The boys' mom and I had decided to move Cody, Caleb, and Cooper to Abilene during the Christmas holidays, and they could transfer schools during the semester break. It seemed like a good idea, but we did not quite make it. About a month before the holidays, something happened that sped up the process.

When we were at the cancer center for a regular post-chemo checkup, something told me to tell the doctor we were ready to sign up for Hospice. Mike had been after me to get that done, but I guess I wanted to continue being superwoman and self-sufficient. The doctor was more than willing to sign the orders, and when I called Robert at Hospice, all he could say was, "It is about time."

That was on a Thursday. On Saturday night, we were still at home, and Jim could not seem to settle down and get a good night's sleep. It was about 1:00 a.m. in the morning when he sat up in bed. He swung his feet over to begin to stand and sat there a few seconds.

I asked, "Are you okay?"

He did not answer.

Slowly, he began to rise. He stood there for a moment and then as he began to turn around to head to the bathroom, he started falling backward. I could not move fast enough. He fell in slow motion, but I could not get there in time. His head crashed into the corner of the bay window.

"NO!" I yelled, as I ran around the bed to him. "Get up, Jim! Please, get up!"

I checked his pulse; he still had a faint one. He was unconscious, but still breathing. I could not get him to wake up. This was not good. Usually if he fell, we could work together and get him up. Not this time. He was over 200 pounds of dead weight. No way could I get him up and back in bed.

What was I to do? I called Hospice first. I explained the situation to the woman who answered, and she said she would call the nurse on duty. In a few minutes, the nurse called to say she and a co-worker were on their way.

I was still trying to be superwoman, but at this point, I didn't know what else to do. I put a pillow under Jim's head and draped a blanket over him. I sat there with him for a few moments, noticing how our room had become quiet. He looked so peaceful lying there, as if asleep. I wanted him to wake up, but I knew he would be out for a while. As I evaluated the situation, I realized I probably would not be able to get him up when he finally did wake. When this realization soaked in, I got up, flipped on my automatic coffee maker, and waited for the Hospice people to arrive.

* * *

In 20 minutes two nurses arrived, and they, too, seemed like angels. When these women walked in the door, I could feel the peacefulness. Their manner was so soft and sweet and calm. I could sense their confidence in their profession, and they reassured me that everything would be fine. Yes, *fine*. This time that word fit the situation.

I offered them coffee and they accepted. I watched as they worked over Jim and checked his vitals. I explained what had happened. I was almost ashamed to tell them the rest of the story…that Jim liked to drink, and sometimes he drank too much. It was an embarrassment for me, even though it was his choice.

I listened to the nurses discuss what to do, and I was not surprised when one of them told me they were going to send for an ambulance. She said that normally they would just get him back in bed, make sure everything was okay and leave, but since he had hit his head, they felt that a doctor needed to be involved.

I was afraid this would be their decision. What was I going to do about the boys? I had to go with Jim to the hospital.

Mike had always told me to call if I needed anything, and now the time had come to take her up on her offer. She answered when I called and said she would be here in a few minutes.

The ambulance arrived, the men hoisted Jim up onto the stretcher, and they wheeled him out the front door. He never knew what was happening. I took the van and followed them to the hospital.

We stayed in a cubicle in the emergency room all night. According to the ER staff, unlike most of the victims who arrived that night, Jim was not a patient who needed immediate critical care. The night seemed endless. I had nothing but hour after hour to dwell on my thoughts while I watched Jim sleep.

I had to come to terms with everything that was happening, and I felt this was a good time to get close to God and search my soul.

I was so *angry*. I wanted to scream, kick, and lash out at anything I could. Life was supposed to be perfect. Until these few hours, I had never actually analyzed how I felt, but now my emotions were bigger than life. I wept. There was nothing I could do to change what was destroying my husband and my family. I could not change the lack of attention from the hospital staffstaff; nor could I choose when we would get to go home. I had no control over how Jim felt, no control over how his declining health was affecting the boys, or how the tumor was eventually going to take Jim's life.

My emotions seemed insurmountable, but I could choose how to deal with them, and how to deal with the precious time Jim and I had left together. It was the longest night of my life, but during those waiting hours, I made some life-altering decisions.

It was time to slow down. Time to quit focusing on all those outside resources I thought would save our lives. Time to focus on Jim, on the boys, and do the things we needed to do for ourselves to get through these next few weeks. It was time to reflect, regroup, get rid of some of the junk, and get back to basics.

It was time to "keep it simple."

Twenty

Jim was awake but disoriented when he was finally released from the hospital. As soon as the emergency room doctor examined Jim, he realized there was no point in ordering X-rays or an MRI. He made a few notes in his chart and told us we could go home.

The Hospice nurses met us at home to help get Jim settled. They bathed and washed him, put on fresh pajamas, and got him back into bed. Then nurses and I sat down at the breakfast table with a pot of coffee to discuss our needs. It was wonderful having Mike there; she had been through this before and she was very soothing and levelheaded. Her presence was incredibly reassuring.

It was early, but the boys began to rouse. After explaining what had happened, I told them to go to the basement and play until I got breakfast ready. However, this was Sunday.

"What, no church?"

"You have it. No church."

"Yay!"

Geez, I loved this house. I could send the four boys to the basement and not hear from them for hours…unless they were hungry.

Since Jim's sight was about gone and his leg muscles had become very weak, we ordered a hospital bed and a wheelchair. I could not leave him alone anymore, so we scheduled a home visit every day for an hour, to allow for freedom. Running had become very sporadic, so Mike and I had joined a small heath club just down the street. While the home health nurse was with Jim, Mike and I could go work out, I could go to the grocery store, or just read a book out on the patio. Everyone agreed that the hour scheduled was a necessity for my well-being.

I called the psychiatrist and cancelled my standing appointments. We quit going to the cancer support meetings, and I gave us permission to stop going to church every time the doors opened. We did not see the chemo doctor anymore, and there were no more trips to the neurosurgeon. I cancelled our appointments with Robert at Hospice, but we agreed to continue our sessions via telephone, as needed. It was time to call the boys' mom. It was time to say goodbye to the triplets. My reign of duty was over.

After the nurses left, I called the boys and fixed them breakfast. Mike was there when I told the boys they would be going to live with their mom. We had talked about this before, so it was no surprise. They knew their dad would die and they would live with their mom. The time had come.

The boys' mom would be there early the next morning to get the boys loaded up and take them to school to check out. Since I was not their legal parent, she would have to do that personally. From there, she would take them directly to Abilene to check them into school. She had rented a three-bedroom apartment, so she was ready. Everyone was ready and everyone understood but Sam. He was devastated.

"She needs to leave us alone!" he screamed.

My heart bled for him. Sam had acquired three little brothers he was very fond of, and they were going to leave just like that. It was not fair. In his opinion, we could all live together and everyone would be fine if she would just leave us alone. He said she had no right to come and get the boys. He would not listen when I tried to tell him I had asked their mom to come. Sam became furious. There was no reasoning with him. He was angrier at that moment than I had ever seen him before, and it was justifiable. His family was being ripped apart and he felt helpless. When he stormed off to his room, Mike gently said, "Let him go. Eventually, he will understand."

It was an endless day. I packed up the boys' belongings as Sam remained rebellious every step of the way. Jim was no help, to say the least, and I felt like the Wicked Witch of the West. Finally, when I could not take anymore, I took Sam to his bedroom and closed the door. I tried to be gentle but firm. His acting like a spoiled child was getting under my skin, and my temper flared. He was going to stop this nonsense before I did something lethal. Where was that little blue pill?

It was so hard to explain to a child how cruel life could be. No matter what I said, nothing eased Sam's pain. I gave him an ultimatum. I told him he could stay in his room, make this possibly the worst day of his life, or he could join us, help us pack, make the best of the situation, and enjoy his brothers' last day here. He stayed in his room a while longer, but eventually came out. He had decided he would be the biggest loser of all if his behavior and attitude continued. Kids can be so insightful when they just put their minds to it.

The triplets handled the situation beautifully. They loved their mom and were ready to go to live with her. Not only were they going to be free of my constant commands, they would not have to eat any more vegetables! They had each other and they would survive. Sam was going to suffer. His brothers were leaving and his future looked dismal. There was nothing I could say or do to make things any better.

Their mother arrived at 7:00 a.m. sharp, and we loaded

everything we could get into her SUV. We had never been big buddies, but I wanted her to know I felt these next few weeks were going to be very difficult for her. I wanted her to know she was very brave and that raising the boys alone was probably going to be the hardest thing she had ever done in her life. I hugged her and told her I would be praying for her.

She held on tightly and whispered, "I'll be praying for you, too."

It's funny…I hadn't needed to take another little blue pill since that day.

Cooper, Caleb, and Cody were gone in a flash. Sam felt the huge void. I tried to explain they would be back very soon. After all, they had to come back to see their dad. Christmas was just around the corner and they would spend some time with us for the holidays. Sam did not go to school that day and I spent most of the morning holding him in my arms. We both cried until we could not cry anymore.

* * *

Christmas! I had not even thought about preparing for our yearly family get-together or even buying presents. What was I going to do? How was I going to shop? I had to think. It was already December 6 and I had not even started shopping. It seemed like a waste of effort, but I could not let Christmas just slip through the cracks. It was my favorite holiday, and if I did not do my best to see that this was a decent Christmas, I would feel cheated. I felt cheated enough already. It was time to call for reinforcements.

I called Dave and Dennie and told them what had happened. I told my pastor, Kathryn, I needed some help. I had to have some sitters to stay with Jim while I went to AA meetings, and I had to have extra sitters for a weekend to get ready for Christmas. I was so grateful to have a church family. Until now, I had thought of the church as Jim's family, but during this time they seemed to have adopted me. I asked for help and they provided.

Dave got busy and put together a schedule for the whole weekend. He had people scheduled to look after Jim for every two hours, starting Friday afternoons. Another dear couple had agreed to stay with him on Thursday nights so I could attend AA. I figured that was one luxury I could not do without. Jim's drinking was no longer an issue since he was mostly immobile, but I needed to keep my sanity. AA does not just keep you sober; it keeps you sane when you think your mind has flown the coop.

It had been a couple of weeks since the boys had moved out, so I emailed their mom and asked if she might be interested in keeping Sam for the weekend. She welcomed the idea. The triplets had missed Sam and had inquired about a visit. This was going to be great. I would have a chance to shop for their presents before they arrived for Christmas.

Since I did not have all the appointments to attend, life became easier. No, not easier, but it was certainly less hectic. The triplets were gone, Jim wasn't drinking anymore, and the days were quiet. Hospice came, Mike and I worked out, I had time to think and more time to spend with Sam. It seemed like the perfect scenario. What was wrong with this picture? My husband was dying. That's what was wrong.

Christmas arrived and the triplets came. Derek stopped by but only stayed a few hours. I could not blame him. Even though I had tried to keep the occasion gay, it was rather dismal. Jon and Josh had moved away but they both managed to come back to town for a brief visit over the holidays. Jim mostly slept, and when he was awake and sitting with us, I never knew if he was aware of his surroundings or if he knew what was going on. It was so sad! He was slipping away, and not one of us could do anything about it.

* * *

Mike spent almost every day with me at home. She came in the mornings to take Sam to school, then she came back a little later to stay until Hospice showed up. We left to work out or run errands, and then she went home for a while. Most evenings, she returned and we ate dinner together. She had become a member of the family. I don't know what we would have done without Mike. She was indispensable.

Jim grew weaker every day. When his eyes were open, he was not seeing. He barely ever spoke, and when he did, the words made no sense. My sweet sparkling-eyed husband was gone. Only his body remained.

Mike began to stay at night. The Hospice nurse had given us some literature on the final days and we knew the time was near. Mike did not want us to be alone. She was with us during that time like a guardian angel, ever present and ever loving. She was God's gift sent to take care of, to nourish, to support, and to pick us up when we fell.

One night, Mike woke me at 4:00 a.m. "Lynette, Jim's breathing has changed."

No! Tears welled up in my eyes as I leapt out of bed. I grabbed the chair we kept in the bedroom for visitors and drew it close to his bed. I reached under the blanket to find his hand. It was so warm.

He cannot be dying now! I wasn't ready for him to go.

It seemed as though he was struggling for every breath, but he seemed so peaceful.

Mike stepped to the other side of the hospital bed. She stroked his hair, and as I looked at her, I saw that halo again. I cried and cried. Death was so near.

Mike called Hospice. The nurses would arrive shortly. Those next few moments should have been frightening, but they were welcome treasures we would store in our memories for a very long time. Mike and I fell quiet. We embraced the time we had left with Jim. We were witnessing life, the heart of the universe, and experiencing the threshold between life and death. I had never felt so close to God.

I leaned over Jim and whispered in his ear, "We love you, Jim."

His breathing stopped.

I stood up and put my arms around him. "We love you so much! Everything will be fine. I promise. Everything will be fine!"

He took one more breath, held it for a second, and let it out slowly. Then, he was gone. *I love you, Jim.*

It was over. The moment was bittersweet, liberating, sad, and surprisingly joyous. I felt incredibly honored to have witnessed such a life. I knew I had been chosen to see Jim's life through to the end, and there was no greater joy than feeling special in that way. God had given me the ultimate gift of taking care of another human being as though it was my only purpose in life.

As Long As Forever

I shall remember you as long,
As there are fields of snow.
And there are flowers in the ground,
That have the strength to grow.
As long as there are stars above,
And moonbeams on the sea.
And just as long as there are songs,
Of love and memory.
I shall remember you today,
And dream of you tonight.
And look for you tomorrow when,
The sun begins to light.
Whatever season month, or year,
This much will be the same.
The only sound of joy will be,
The mention of your name.
I shall remember you as long,
As there are earth and sky.
And all the time eternity,
May take to say good-by.

Love,
Jim

Epilogue

It has been over a year now since Jim died on that cold day in January, and the time has not gone by without pain. *How are you doing? I'm fine...NOT.* I tried to kid myself, but I was not fine. I was exhausted, both mentally and physically, and I did not know who I was. For two years, I had been a nanny and a caregiver, and then all of a sudden, I was just Sam's mom.

I had not been "fine" until just recently. Only this time, I really am fine. Part of my recovery has taken place through writing this book. Now, I understand. I see things clearly. "Why me?" is not a question I ask anymore. I know why. All along, my brief time with Jim, Cooper, Caleb, and Cody had been God's plan.

After losing two fathers, Sam has been through more in his young life than most adults have. He learned how to open his heart and love the triplets as if they were his blood brothers. He grew to adore Jim and accept him as his own father. Sam experienced the joys of having a real family, only to have it jerked right out from under him. He was angry and hurt, and he grieved for quite some time. But his resilience is truly God given. Sam is going to be okay.

AA teaches us that God will not give us anything we cannot handle. I know I could not have made it without Him. Before Jim and the boys, I only thought I knew God. He is my life now; I depend on Him for everything.

So what am I thinking now after marrying a man with triplets? God gave me an opportunity that not many people get to experience. He put three little boys in my care so that I could teach them what they needed to learn, and so I could learn what they needed to teach me. Today I have a deep understanding of love, tolerance, patience, forgiveness, and acceptance. God also allowed me to take care of a very special man for the last years of his life. I have received these gifts that only God can give.

Jim's boys live with their mother now, and last I heard, they are all doing fine. Maybe the triplets don't eat vegetables anymore, but at least they know what they are!

*Special thanks to the Three C's
for touching my life.*

Author's Note

I started writing this memoir for therapy back when Jim was diagnosed with the tumor. I stopped and started many times, then finally found some healing and finished this book about a year after he passed. That was over 16 years ago in February of 2005.

After Jim passed, Mike decided it was time to move to Tennessee to be close to her children and grandchildren. Her duty was done as a guide for me. Her house sold within a month, and she was gone. You see, she showed up in my life for a reason. Just like Kathryn, Bobby, Sarah, Dennie and Dave, and all the other people who helped us through. They were Heaven-sent angels, and I am grateful to all of them.

Sam visited the triplets a few times in Abilene, and Cody, Caleb, and Cooper came to stay with us some. Eventually, we lost touch with Jim's kids. We all got busy with our own lives, and life kept moving on.

After school was out that year, Sam and I took off to see Tennessee and my dear friend, Mike. As we were pulling out of the driveway, Sam asked, "Mom, do you feel like you have just gotten rid of a ball and chain?" I understood what he meant, referring to the enormous emotional weight I had carried over the last tragic year. I thought that was pretty deep for a ten-year-old. We had a wonderful trip.

When we returned home to Lubbock, my heart felt lightened. It was time for Sam and I to fully move on. I decided to try another internet search on a matchmaker site. God must have been shining down on me then, letting me know I was ready to love someone new. Instantly, I found the next love of my life, and a new chapter that I am still living today with my husband, Jerry. He worked in the oil industry and I got a teaching job. We married, worked until retirement, then sold our house, and moved to a golf resort in Central Texas.

Now, let me tell you the rest of the story…

After I finished the book, I sought a publisher. I sent the first three chapters with a cover letter to probably about two dozen editors over a few years, and I received some very nice rejections! However, I got discouraged and stopped the pursuit. When I got a teaching job, I gave up the chance of ever publish my sweet story.

A few months ago, my husband, Jerry, was out talking to a neighbor, and he explained how his wife was publishing a book herself. Jerry came home and relayed the information. This sparked my curiosity, so I started researching self-publishing. I knew there was a possibility but was still very skeptical.

That very evening, my son, Sam, who is now a young man, called out of the blue. He was so excited! "Mom, guess who just called me?" I named a few guesses, but he finally blurted out, "Cody!"

I was shocked. I knew Sam was active on social media, but I hadn't heard from any of the triplets for many, many years. Cody, now a young man as well, called me that night. We had a nice long discussion about life with Jim, the illness, and the sorrow of losing him to cancer. Cody told me he was now a phlebotomist, Caleb an electrical engineer and married, and Cooper had joined the marines. I couldn't be happier for those boys! I told Cody I had written a book about the whole ordeal years ago, and he was eager to read it. I sent the raw manuscript to him immediately via email.

The very next day, I had lunch with a few friends and told them the story. They were all very interested. Since we had only moved to this area five years ago, no one really knew about my past. Sam and I had moved on and lived our new life with Jerry, and I barely thought about my book anymore.

However, one of the ladies is a retired creative writing teacher, and she offered to take a look at my unpublished memoir. She was concerned about our friendship, so she said, "I will only do this if I can be very honest, and it will not damage our relationship."

I quickly said, "Sure!" I was anxious for her to read my book and give me some insight.

A few days later, she called, and when I saw the caller ID, I did not answer. My heart started racing, and I wasn't sure if I wanted to hear the bad news. Here was her message:

"Hi, Lynette, this is Betsy. I have finished your delightful book, and we need to talk!"

Oh, my! What a wonderful message! I was shaking as I picked up the phone. A few minutes later I summoned the courage to call her. (I did not want her to know I was screening my calls.)

So, I called. Betsy informed me that there was a book editor living in our community who helped writers publish their story. What? Yes, he was the son of a lady I played bridge with, so I waited a few days and then gave her a call. I was in a quandary. I was loving my retired life, playing bridge, golf, going out to lunch with ladies, directing the new hand-bell choir, attending church services and bible studies, and so many other activities that are available when you have grandchildren and live in a wonderful community—lake, boat, swimming pools, etc. I knew if I wanted to pursue this new self-publishing adventure, it would mean WORK for me, and I had given up on that a few years earlier.

I met with my friend's son, Brian. I gave him the only hard copy which I had picked up from Betsy earlier that day. Brian and I had a wonderful discussion about my story, and the possibilities of editing. I walked away feeling very positive.

During this most recent journey, I have struggled. I have prayed to God to guide me. I have tried to add to the story describing my intimate encounters, and I have changed some of the more questionable passages. I managed to finish the revised manuscript, and then I sent it to Brian to potentially edit my book and assist me with self-publishing.

I had very mixed feelings. I was looking forward to making this story even better, but it had been very emotional for me. Also, I couldn't resist paying attention to the signs. I am a "signs" person. I watch for red flags and green lights.

A few weeks later, Brian called and I did not screen the phone call. He was so excited about the possibility of getting my memoir ready to publish! He sent me all of his information, including the timeline for self-publishing and the cost. Wait. I had to think about this. Was I willing to WORK? Again, I sought God for an answer and here we are.

I hope you have enjoyed reading this memoir as much as I have enjoyed working on it, in spite of all the nearby distractions. It has taken a little more time than expected, and I would not have finished if it had not been for the constant encouragement from my husband, Jerry. Let me give a huge shout-out to Jerry. After Jim died, once again, I landed on the internet to find my second (or third, or fourth) great love. It did not take long. God knew I needed someone else to love, and despite all the "signs," I found him! Jerry has been so instrumental in his willingness to help me succeed, so now I believe...while the third time could have been the charm, the fourth time is even better! I absolutely love being married to Jerry, plus, he's healthy! I know, because I made him take a physical before we got married.

I also want to thank all my friends who were so supportive and helped me get to the finish line. Thank you to everyone who helped me make this book happen.

About the Author

Lynette Moore is a retired certified teacher of Art, Mathematics, and Career Technology and Education. Before retiring from teaching, she taught English as a second language, was a well-known piano teacher, and served as the music director of a small church in West Texas. Heavily involved in church music throughout her life, she is now co-director of the handbell choir at her church and has instructed young people in playing handbells and chimes. This is her debut book.

She and her current husband, Jerry, live in a quiet Central Texas resort community where they enjoy golf, social events, and lake living. Lynette also plays bridge, holds yoga classes at her home, loves Bible study, and just people in general.

CPSIA information can be obtained
at www.ICGtesting.com
Printed in the USA
BVHW081155080222
628386BV00001B/150